Children of Autumn

Children of Autumn

Autism – Here on Purpose

By Grace Kohn

"Shit Happens, and Then Shift Happens"

I dedicate this book to my two beautiful kids,
Griffin and Julianne Shea:
my greatest teachers,
my children of autumn.

I love you,

Mom

For those who have eyes to see the magic in the mess

Table of Contents

"Shit Happens, and Then Shift Happens" .... *v*

Acknowledgements ....*xi*

Autism: Light. Ignite. .... *xv*

Preface: How The Book Came About ....*xix*

Introduction *1*

Chapter 1—Mystical Beginnings *5*

Chapter 2—Here And Now: What Do We Do Now? *19*

Chapter 3—Expanding The Healing: Introducing Jonathan Alderson and IMTI *33*

Chapter 4—Healing The Gut *45*

Chapter 5—Attitudinal Tools: How To Empower Yourself *53*

Chapter 6—Family Of Light: Here To Help Our Earth *63*

Chapter 7—Fun(d)raising Techniques *71*

Chapter 8—Trust Yourself *75*

Afterword *87*

Acknowledgements

Without the following special souls, you would not be reading this book, Julianne would not be skiing up a storm, or reading, horseback riding or smiling as much as she does. We really couldn't have made it without you, so "Thank you." Two words that mean I am grateful to each and every one of you for your support and love. You are a miracle, you contributed to a miracle, and I wish you many miracles today and always.

To my family of light, my Haka family and SRT Sisterhood: You are always with me, wherever I go. I feel your blessings and radiance. Thank you so much. Shine on: Kim Wallace, Sharon and Gord Anderson, Travis Anderson and Courtney Mayhew, Johnny Gids, Anika Gideon-Zoth, Hugh and Kathy Juncker, Sue Gehrig, Keith Doll, Bill and Anne Little, Regena Bergen, Danielea Castell, Glenda and Bob Thompson, Laurel McKirdy, Ingrid Heise, Paula Klassen, Maureen Allard, Al and Sandy Birnie, Lynda and Jamin Knight, Parise Cyr-Lasonder, Margo Bereska, Marga Wierenga, Desha Bene, Claude Poirier, Susan Carolla, Elise Brathwaite, Toby Davidson, Alec Steinwall, Andrea Scholz, Megan Hughes, Helen Anderson , Jody Hoel, Rhonda Ann Clarke, Peter Boyne, Maggie McDowell, Ginny Larkin, Ose Kolman, The Hokkanen family, Anna Marie, Marie-Helene Hamel, Bob and Nicole Covey, Marianne and Alfred Kong, Edwin Richard, John L'Hirondelle, Ellen Torstenson Myras, Gretchen Hickmott, Gord Fielding, Gregory Deagle, Guillermo Rivera, Heidi Farrell, Inha Lu, Jeanette and Lynn Nelson, Jessy Dion, Josh Dennis, Kory Wueshner, Susie Pollard, Lilia M, Lu Livermore, Marion Berard, Nancy and Andy Furrer, Nicole Hartley Bradford, Nicole Pomerleau, Nita and Walt Ludwick, Philip Bradley Krause, Sandra Hodge, Valerie Plante and

Robert Pearman, JoAnn Henningson, Marilyn Stacey, Angela Tsounis and Jacinta Broemeling.

To my Sisterhood of the Travelling Green Umbrellas: We have been together a very long time. Thank you for being my laughter, my reprise, my support, my "base". I love you all: Sandy Halim, Laura Blaney, Barbara Tong and Donna Delfosse. May we continue to gather, well into our 100s. I look forward to each and every upcoming adventure!

To all the wonderful therapists who worked with Julianne along the way, every minute contributed to her healing. You are the reason she can do what she can do. Thank you and Bless you all: Peggy Plato, Denise Brosch, Brenda Hill, Christa Bergeron, Ward Hughson, Crystal Rhayn, Sandra Druyff-Olsen, Heidi Schaefer, Sarah Ferguson, Christina Gomez (surrogate Grandma), Marciana Lipnica, Lucy Gada, Jonathan Alderson, Jonathan Rivero, Lena Martin, Les and Keslin Dolan, Melanie Shupe, Melody Gaboury, Olivia Waterhouse, Tanya Lipscomb, Erin Brett, Kim MacDonald, Kyle Darroch, Jessica Simpson, Angelie Torreon, Jessica, Carla Slover, Jovi Russell, Jen Russell, Carly Melanson, Leanne Cross and Alan Shiveral.

To my partner, David Wensley, for his understanding and support of this project, his ability to restabilize me when I'm feeling unbalanced and his generosity and kindness: You are my "Jesus".

To all the people who donated their time, money and resources to this project. May you receive the gifts of generosity tenfold: Linda Drecun, Liz Olsen, Lynda Olson, Marianne Garrah, Dave Baker, Marylou Weiner, Maude Prezeau, Pamela Griffiths, Paul Hoefgen, Randal Riddell, Shawnee Janes-Wilson, Wendy Niven, Nancy Sierchio, Lois Van Koughnet, Pamela Jeck, Val and

Morley Fleming, Dr. Laureen DiStefano, Ursula Winkler, Don and Marilyn Campbell, Sue and Al Cesco, Tony Pearce, Bruno and Earla Ritter, Sheona Ayles, Noella and Lou Lazarri, Christine James–Blondell, Marie Ludwick, The Bronskill family, Nelda Edwards, Margot Simpson, Keri Arnold, Mona Ismaeil, Cindy Friedrich, The Jasper Healthcare Foundation, Al and Karen Bain, The Turcott family, Willow Jones, The Mahler family, The Scott family, Karen Huculuk, Tekarra Color Lab, Kelly and Jurgen Reed, The Baxters, The Tassoni family, The Kennedys, Dave Prockiw, Karen and Ron St. Martin, Val and Doug Witwicky, Vicki Wallace, Marmot Ski Hill, Anna Scott, Steph Dolan, Beth Russell and the hundreds of people who came to an Improv night, a Music benefit, or bought a valentine cookie, donated their bottles for us to recycle or bought a ticket for a raffle. If you contributed even a dollar to this project we are thankful for your support.

And finally to Rob Cuesta and everyone at BrightFlame Books who helped to make this book a reality.

Hundreds of people contributing to a miracle in motion. Hundreds of people helping one child. This is the "Awe" in Autism. This is the light in the dark. This is Love. I cried every time I received.

Thank you from the bottom, top and sides of my very thankful Heart!!!

Namaste

Grace

Autism: Light. Ignite.

Twenty-two years ago, walking towards the grocery store with my then one-year-old son, I received a song. I say I "received" a song because I had no intention of writing a song, nor had I ever written a song. As someone who loves to sing, I do often have a song "playing" from my mouth, so to speak, and this day was no different. What was different, however, was that this song coming out of my mouth—this song which brought me to tears as I sang the bridge—did not exist. At least not on Earth. At least not up until that point.

And I realized very quickly that this song had somehow come through me, as fully formed music and words. From where or from whom, I still do not know to this day. What I do know is that this song has become my life's work, and part of that body of work will include this book. Children of Autumn speaks "of a people who had come long ago. They were sent from above and back here to help me/us to be free."

Two years later I gave birth to a very healthy beautiful baby girl named Julianne. We call her Jewels. Jewels has autism. Statistically, she is one of the one in every sixty-eight people on Earth living with autism. Today Julianne is twenty years old. Those twenty years were the MOST challenging time of my life. But, the lessons I learned from being engaged with Julianne's growth have been the most powerful.

At a certain point in her development, I had an epiphany: I realized that although I was doing everything in my power to help this child grow, she most certainly was helping me also. This understanding grew, and became the reason for this book.

I believe children with autism are here to help us grow. When I say "grow", I mean to increase our light. Growing up with my daughter was the greatest initiation a person could go through. I did things people would squirm at because of her, but all for love.

Oh, it was tough. Trust me; I wasn't a saint all the time. But, because I loved—and love—her so much, I would not give up on doing everything I possibly could to help her excel. Along the way, I worked with many extraordinary people, some of whom I will introduce to you. I will share with you the strategies we used to help Julianne grow; the attitudinal tools I learned that will keep anyone happy and energetic even in the face of doom (Some of them can even be utilized in a bank lineup!).

I changed a lot over these twenty years and renounced many beliefs that were hurting not just me but also our very own Mother Earth. I was scared but always found support. I cried a lot but always stopped. I believe I am a much more loving person now thanks to having both my children and the experiences I had with Jewels.

I believe these kids are jewels, here to help us save ourselves and, in the process, our Earth. The tools I learned from working with my daughter are what grew my light from one that was fading to one that is lit. These tools, I now wish to share with you. Whether you are a parent, a grandparent or a caregiver of a child with autism, this book will help you.

Twenty-two years ago, when I first heard the Children of Autumn song, it was the line in the bridge that burst my dam (so to speak): "The light in you had started to fade." When I first heard these words I knew they were true, and I knew I had to make a change. These words were my wake-up call to reclaiming that which I truly am—light. By having allowed myself the space to fuel it and grow it into an incredible torch, I believe I can be a guide for others to do the same. Being with autism was my greatest teacher. It still is.

My hope is that our journey will help you also to grow your light. May we one day unite and light up our world with hope. The song "We're gonna start a revolution" continues to play in my brain. My intention is that upon reading this book, the "belief" that birthing a child with autism is some sort of death sentence will change to a knowing that you have been gifted one of the greatest journeys of all time: a chance to reconnect with your truth, your power, your spirit.

May these words and ideas bless you and your child.

[xviii] *Grace Kohn*

Preface: How The Book Came About

HOLY SHIT!!!

I will never forget the first time it happened.

I was asleep in bed (and I am a very deep sleeper), but over a course of time, it was as if waves of 'smell stink' were drifting over my nose and waking me up. Each waft was waking me up a little more. I thought to myself, "What is that? It's not bacon."

I woke up, climbed out of bed, opened the door to my room and crossed the hall. I opened the door to Julianne's bedroom and there in front of me sat my beautiful daughter covered in poo from head to toe. It was in her mouth, her eyes, her hair, all over her entire body. It was on the sheets, her duvet, the carpet, the drapes, the windows, her toys. It was everywhere!!! It was incredible, and I mean this genuinely, for I had no emotion. I felt no anger, no sadness, no feelings of self-pity, no frustration, no fear—only AWE.

Of course, I had never seen anything like this before; never knew something like this could even occur. But, here we were, and I was literally in awe. It was as if time had stopped for a moment and everything was okay. What I was observing just "was". There was no judgment; there was no pain. It was what it was—clearly a room full of shit between my daughter and me.

In a way, it has become a metaphor for me: her shit, my shit. It has been a healing process, a "clean-up" of all our shit. I stood in that doorway for what seemed like a very long time. I had an incredible sense of lightness in my

XX] *Grace Kohn*

body. I almost felt like something was allowing me to experience what an enlightened perspective on this type of situation could be. I cherished that experience and used it many times later as a guidepost for what is possible. After moments of observing the situation, I began the four-hour clean-up job required.

There would be many more of these occurrences in the years to come, in various locations all over our home. Many of them wouldn't be so "pretty" regarding my response, but ALWAYS I would experience them as a potential to reach for again. Because I had experienced this type of "awe" once, I knew it existed and forever it would be somewhere in my body. If I wanted, and if I so chose, I could access this type of response again.

I played the victim many times after this. That, too, is okay because that was my choice. But, what I learned about myself along the way—and how many conscious changes I made to my thinking—is why I am writing this book. All this caca I dealt with became my greatest catalyst for growth and healing. Yes, it was difficult. Yes, I cried and screamed many tears and many profanities. I cursed God and blamed Him/Her for all that was happening to me. I felt sorry for myself time and time again. On some level I believed deep down I must be a truly evil person: I deserved all this shit, this was my Karma. God, what had I done in a past life to deserve this? And on and on it went.

Then I learned an excellent technique from a fantastic place, and my life began to change. And my daughter started to change. We both changed so much that I knew that, when the shit literally occurred, if I did my work I would find a gem in all of it… a Jewel.

I always knew, and still do.

Introduction

Have you ever heard of the Eye of God or the Eye of Ra? Have you ever seen that amazing picture taken from a Hubble telescope that looks like an enormous eye in the sky? When I was pregnant with my daughter, I had one of the most extraordinary experiences I have ever had. It made me question my rational mind. It was definitely of an esoteric nature. I had to phone a good friend of mine to make sure I was of sound mind, which she convinced me I was (some are still debating!). In hindsight, I should have known it was a foreshadowing of what was coming, but I didn't know what was coming, so I didn't make any deductions at the time. The only thing I knew for sure was something unique and strange had occurred. Where it would lead, only time would tell. And it did.

As a baby in utero, my daughter Julianne felt very "strong" to me. I remember thinking *this is a genius in here*. Five years later, she was misdiagnosed as mentally retarded. Two years after that she was re-diagnosed as a person with autism. When she was born, she was graded a 10 on the Apgar scale; she was a beautiful baby, alert and seemingly making contact with people from the get-go. Around the time children typically start to speak, Julianne remained silent. Her eyes were so incredibly bright, though. And, the way she seemed to take in every situation, I couldn't yet bring myself to think that there might be something wrong with her. Besides, her dad was a near genius (if not a genius) and, according to his mother, he didn't speak until he was four years old. But by three years old, it was clear that there was a vast developmental delay between Julianne and her peers.

Just for the record, her father and I chose not to vaccinate her, so that debate does not enter into our story. After numerous rounds of testing, with years in between, Julianne finally—at age seven—was awarded the proper diagnosis of autism. With a proper diagnosis now in hand, the real work began. Jewel's feces-smearing antics were increasing, and at seven years old she could do little more that murmur a few words, watch TV and eat with her hands. The school she was attending didn't know how to help her, and I ended up taking a two-year sabbatical so that I could work with her myself.

We began our journey into connecting with her by learning great tools from the Options Institute in Massachusetts. We converted our basement into a playroom and learning area for Jewels. We inspired and trained volunteers, sharing experiences at group meetings held once a week at our home. "Be the Miracle" from the movie Bruce Almighty became our mantra. We witnessed an enormous miracle within the first month of working with Jewels as she said one thousand words that we documented. From someone who might say two to three words in a day, this was astonishing; it certainly turbo-boosted us into maintaining focus for the years to come. The Options Institute truly is a place where miracles do come true. An introduction to this beautiful place and some stories of my experiences there are included in this book.

From the Options Institute, we were blessed by the appointment of Jonathan Alderson to our team. Jonathan had worked with the Options Institute for many years and was venturing back to Canada to start up his company called IMTI (Intensive Multi-Treatment Intervention). He had already worked with over two thousand families who had been involved with autism and held the belief that, although what the Options Institute was offering families was valuable, there were more components to the healing of this disorder that could be tried.

We fundraised the monies to bring him to our beautiful "middle of nowhere" home in Jasper, Alberta, and in this book, I will share many of our "fun(d)raising" techniques with you.

His leadership catapulted Julianne from only being able to perform a minimal number of tasks, enabling her to open doors into her developmental abilities in every area. He has become like family to us now. His love and commitment to making life better for everybody on this journey are complete.

This book includes teachings from Jonathan for your child, and for you; on how to stay "attitudinally fit" to stay on course. He opened our minds to the idea that the gut (literally) of our friends with autism probably needs some attention. There is much research now on how the health of the gut can and does dramatically affect the functioning of our brains. I will share with you where we were led on this subject by Jonathan and by the wisdom of other experts on this subject.

Living with autism is not an easy road. It has been the most challenging period I have experienced to date. But, it also fuelled the most personal evolution for me that this timeframe could allow. As a result of everything that occurred with my daughter, I have changed, I am a better person: I know I am.

Me being a better person is good for our Earth—this I also know to be true. This understanding has led me to a very esoteric idea of why autism is here in the first place (Oh, it's way "out there", folks!) but it makes total sense to me. I share this ideology with you in these upcoming pages.

My hope is that my understanding of autism will help you to breathe easier and trust yourself more. In this day and age, it is my belief that we must all wake up to the idea that we can think intelligently for ourselves. Ultimately, we must learn to trust ourselves and the choices we make for ourselves, for the people we love, and for our Earth. This book concludes with different stories that taught me that I can, in fact, honour myself and am worthy of doing so.

Ultimately, Julianne reawakened my ability to see and experience AWE. Watching a child take 4 ½ years to learn how to tie her shoelaces, to ski down a hill in perfect balance and to speak after seven years of silence rewired me. Add to this the fact that I started "seeing things in the dark" and receiving channelled songs from somewhere "out there", it sparked my wonder. This condition of autism is not coincidentally named; I just think they spelled it wrong: AWE-'tis-(th)EM. This describes it more accurately. At least to me.

These children are here for a reason. They are right on time. They are asking us to WAKE UP. They are asking us to change. Trust me that—even though sometimes you may feel like you are jumping off a cliff into an abyss— you will not fall: you will fly!

Surround yourself with a solid team or 'family' as I call them (you'll read more about this in Chapter 6). Not only will you make it through this, but you will also evolve beyond even your imaginings. I swear to you, if I was able to make it through this journey and be in the place I am today, you can too. Just believe (even a tiny bit) that you will be blessed as a result of this child, and I promise you, you will. It is my intention to share with you everything that woke me up and keeps me awake. God Bless you on this journey. You are NOT alone; you are in the company of Angels.

Chapter 1—Mystical Beginnings

"Children of Autumn, they were sent from Above. Smiling and carefree they were laughing at me, For I was crying and hoping someday I'd be free; Someday I'd be me."

These words make up the chorus of the song I received in 1994, two years before Julianne arrived on Earth.

Wednesday morning, 7:30 a.m. My young son and his dad leave the house. A "voice" guides me to go downstairs to the CD player and select a specific piece of music. Then, as my six-month-pregnant self is swaying to the music, a series of unexplainable events occurs. These events, coupled with other experiences involving Julianne, led me to create a belief about why autism is growing at the speed of lightning.

In the early 2000s, one in every one thousand people was diagnosed with this disorder. Today it is one in every sixty-eight people, and according to some predictions, the rate will continue to increase. Why this is occurring, I believe is no coincidence. I honestly think these beings are here on purpose.

How I came to this belief makes up the rest of this chapter.

Who are these people and why are they here? Dare I ask where they came from? People with autism can be found everywhere on our planet today. They can be great teachers for us if we choose to understand what they are teaching. With understanding, our perception of them can substantially change. Changing one's attitude can lead to more peace and ultimately more healing for everyone involved: parents, caregivers and the child itself. One of the reasons these kids are here is to heal; and not just themselves. My understanding of these people is that they have the capacity to do great things. Having witnessed many wonders, I have much to share.

And for the record, I'm not crazy.

Okay, maybe just a little.

The CD I was guided to put on was Dionne Warwick. The exact song which was playing, I will reveal later. As I was dancing to her beautiful voice, sunlight started to stream through our stained glass window. I bathed in that light. It was a peaceful experience.

Baby and mom were enjoying a moment of calm. And then I saw it. This enormous eye, about the size of a football, entered my mind's screen. My rational mind immediately questioned what I was seeing. *What is that?* I thought to myself. *It is your angel,* I heard an inner voice say. I fell to the ground and wept.

Now, let me start by telling, I have never done any drugs in this lifetime. Never even tried marijuana. Personally, I don't care if you partake in recreational drugs, but for the purpose of this story, I have to tell you I have never done any hallucinogenic drugs. Never tried peyote. Nor have I participated in Ayahuasca.

What I saw that morning was with my natural sight. Once the tears stopped falling, I looked up.

We had an open concept living room/dining room area. There standing on my dining room table was an Eagle, illuminated in light. Just to be clear, the Eagle was made of light, and it was in *my* house. Of course, I thought I was going crazy. Later I was to learn there are different levels of consciousness, and what I was witnessing was what was going on in the Light realms. Pretty trippy to say the least. Beautiful, though, and fascinating.

I sat on the floor for a while and then phoned a dear friend of mine who had some experience with these types of occurrences. She helped me process. Then I phoned my "wasbund". He was quite calm about the story I told him and said, "Let's just see what happens."

What I realized that morning was how much we don't see and how much we can learn to see. I knew intuitively that this occurrence had something to do with the baby I was carrying inside. Little did I know what was coming down the chute for us. God (and don't you go running away now just because I dropped the "G" word) has a way of communicating with us. (P.S. If God is too loaded a word for you, we can use Spirit).

So what did the eye represent? Where did it come from? What does it have to do with my baby? My life?

Along my journey, it has sparked many paths of interest. Once, when I was working with a healer with Julianne, Dwaine—the healer—asked me if I believed in Angels. "Yes," I said and proceeded to tell him the story I just told you. He leaned in really close to me and, almost in a whisper, said into my ear, "The Eye; The Eye of Ra."

I didn't know what he meant, but apparently my emotional body did. I had another cathartic cry—and let me assure you there was NO WAY I could have held back those tears. It was as if a dam had been broken wide open. Again some form of remembering was occurring.

According to Wikipedia, in Ancient Egyptian mythology, the Eye of Ra *"functions as a feminine counterpart to the sun god Ra and a violent force that subdues his enemies."* The Eye is both an extension of Ra's power and an independent entity that *"acts as mother, sibling, consort and daughter of the sun god. She is his partner in the creative cycle in which he begets the renewed form of himself that is born at dawn."*[1]

Interestingly, as I was editing this book, the Dionne Warwick song that I was guided to way back in 1994 came to me again (remember, I said I'd reveal what it was later in the book? Well, "later" is now!). I found myself singing "I sing at Dawn". Just saying…

Does the eye I saw when I was pregnant with Jewels have anything to do with this? One never knows for sure, but along the way there most certainly have been signs indicating that somehow I have a connection with Egypt and Julianne has been a catalyst for me rediscovering these links.

Judy Satori, author of *Sunshine Before the Dawn*, also speaks of The Eye of God. According to her, "Everything is created by the Eternal Eye of God and the geometric shape of a pyramid." Julianne enjoys listening to Judy Satori's work. From the first time she came across Judy, she was clearly drawn to her. Furthermore, as a result of both Judy's and Kathleen McGowan's work (author of *The Expected One*, and *The Book of Love*), both Julianne and I have visited Chartres Cathedral twice as well as Sainte Baume, the cave where it is said Mary Magdalene lived for twenty years. Interestingly, connections are also being drawn in popular literature between Mary Magdalene and Egypt.

We made four separate trips up to the cave during our visit to Southern France in 2013. There are many beautiful stories about our experiences there that we will share with you one day. In the meantime, please see our blog at www.childrenofautumn.com for some highlights.

---

[1] https://en.wikipedia.org/wiki/Eye_of_Ra

In hindsight, I feel as though both the Eye that I saw on this peculiar morning, and the Eagle, were messages given to me by Spirit. These symbols began a weaving that would continue throughout my life. When I read Ina Woolcott's article *Eagle Power Animal, Symbol of Spirit, Vision and Strength* on ShamanicJourney.com, I understand why an eagle landed in my dining room on that special day.

Listen to what she says: "Eagle's medicine includes swiftness, strength, courage, wisdom, keen sight, illumination of Spirit, healing, creation, knowledge of magic, ability to see hidden spiritual truths, rising above the material to see the spiritual, ability to see the overall pattern/big picture, connection to spirit guides and teachers and higher truths, great power and balance, dignity and grace, intuitive and creative spirit, respect for the boundaries of the regions, grace achieved through knowledge and hard work. Eagle feathers assist medicine people/shamans in connecting with Spirit for healing. They are deemed the most sacred healing tools, a symbol of power, healing and wisdom."

Furthermore, she writes, "The eagle is also linked to the sun in Gaelic lore, having been called in the Gaelic language Suil-na-Greine, Eye of the Sun." Finally, she explains, "From Eagle we learn that life looks different from an aerial perspective. We need to take a new view of the challenges in our lives. If we don't readily find solutions, it may be because our vision is too limited to see the solutions that are so glaringly obvious.

According to Woolcott, Eagle teaches us that solutions are not always intellectual. Eagle's teaching is about looking beyond intellect to access both intelligence and Spirit. It's about stepping back and looking at the bigger picture; learning from the past and present while looking to the future and letting go of old restricting beliefs that are holding us back.

> *"Eagle teaches us to face courageously our fear of the unknown, so we are then able to fly as high as our heart's joy can take us. Eagle is also linked with courage. To give up our limited perspectives, to release ourselves from comfortable, familiar thought patterns, even when they don't appear to be working, and fly into a larger world requires that we are brave enough to enter unknown realms."*

Later, she tells us, "Those with this power animal are shown how to master the art of patience in every area of their life. For within the energy of patience, all things are possible. Eagle teaches us how to go through life without becoming attached to anything, how to accept what comes our way and see everything as a gift from the universe. With their acute hearing they hunt as much by ear as by sight. If eagle soars into your life, the ability to hear spiritually and psychically will awaken."

So what does it mean when Eagle comes in to our life?

> *"With Eagle as your power animal, you feel the need to have an involvement with creation, a willingness to experience extremes, a willingness to use your abilities, a willingness to seek out your true emotions. You must become much more than you ever imagined would be possible. Eagle symbolizes a state of being that is reached through inner work, understanding and passing the initiation tests that come about from reclaiming our personal power. Eagle is the gift of clear vision with which one can truly see, to live in*

balance with heaven and Earth. Eagle shows you how to look above so you can touch Grandfather Sun with your heart, to love the Shadow as much as the Light.

You are being asked to give yourself permission to be free to reach the joy that your heart longs for."²

OH, MY GOD!!! If I had known how to speak Eagle when this incredible bird landed on my dining room table, I would have had a glimpse of what the next twenty years was going to look like. Everything Ina talks about is exactly why I am writing this book. Did I learn patience? Yes! To let go of Judgements? Absolutely! Am I more free and joyous based on the new beliefs I grew and nurtured because of my interactions with autism? 100% Correct!

What an exciting, incredible EXPERIENCE this meeting with my Eagle was, considering Julianne was still in utero. It is true: God/Spirit speaks in unusual ways. I am learning to speak Eagle. I have passed through a great initiation. I am here to help you with yours.

Who Are You, Little One?

As much as I became a teacher for Julianne, she also was and is one for me. From the very beginning, Julianne was involved in me experiencing AWE-some moments. Whether she was consciously aware of what she was doing, we will never know, but she was always there connected with these occurrences.

---

² http://www.shamanicjourney.com/eagle-power-animal-symbol-of-spirit-vision-and-strength

On one visit to Toronto, Ontario, Julianne—then aged three—her brother Griffin, and I were shopping in a New Age bookstore. A girlfriend of mine had given me a gift certificate for this store as a birthday present. I had $40 to spend and I was looking for the latest book (at the time) by Barbara Marciniak, called *Family of Light: Pleiadian Tales and Lessons in Living*. I was looking and looking but wasn't having much luck. Griffin was asking me if he could have a book about animal spirit guides, some crystals, and a drumming CD, and Jewels was running in and out of the aisles.

I did find a book by Neale Donald Walsch, *The Little Soul and the Sun*, which I highly recommend by the way. As I picked this book up, that little voice in my head spoke again. *Buy it*, it said repeatedly. I remember the cost clearly; it was $26.00 (which at that time was a lot of money for me to pay for a book). *Buy it*, the voice prompted. Well, since I wasn't finding *The Family of Light*, I told Griffin he could pick out one thing and with the balance of the gift certificate I would buy the Neale Donald Walsch book. We proceeded to the checkout—book and drumming CD in hand—paid, and left the store. Just outside, Jewels—nearly three at this time—indicated to me that she had to go the bathroom. She didn't speak, but I knew she had to go, so back to the store we wandered. We used the facilities, washed our hands and headed for the exit. Jewels, however, took an alternative route. She walked up to a particular shelf, pulled out a book, and gave it to me. As I looked at the cover, a strange feeling filled my body. There in my hands was *The Family of Light*. Coincidence? I think not. And you can bet your bottom dollar, I hadn't been wandering around telling my children, "I'm looking for a book; it's called the Family of Light."

No. This incident, like so many to follow, led me to ask the question, *Who are you little one? And where did you come from?* Of course, I had to purchase the book. More foreshadowing of what was on the horizon.

Where Does Autism Come From?

Why are so many children being diagnosed with autism these days? I do have a theory … Hold onto your seat folks, because it most definitely is "out there".

I have done a lot of work with my daughter over the past thirteen years. I have been to many conferences, classes, doctors, alternative therapists, and I have met many parents and therapists who work with children who have autism. Based on the people I have met, their stories and how I have observed them go to great lengths to help these people coupled with the mystical experiences I have had with my own daughter, I have come to believe that these particular children are not here by coincidence.

There are many theories as to why autism is so prevalent today, and honestly I do think many of them hold a piece to the puzzle. There is, of course, the vaccination argument, and I have heard stories that brought me to tears: children who were "typical" and then after receiving their full set of shots regressed to such a point where they couldn't speak anymore or even look at their parents, and were very uncomfortable in their bodies. In our case, we did not vaccinate Julianne, so it is not the reason for her autism.

Then there is the theory that our environment—our pollution, our food sources, even our water—is affecting these children negatively. I have heard them compared to the canaries in the coal mines, coming here to tell us, "your earth is in trouble, and you need to stop and change and heal." Most of us recognize that there are problems with our environment, and many groups are addressing these issues. I do believe that this message is part of their reason for being here.

My perspective, however, goes a little further, and is perhaps a bit more woo woo. I mentioned at the opening of this book that I received a song twenty-two years ago. I will reiterate that I had no intention of writing a song, nor had ever written a song. The song that so effortlessly came out of my mouth has these lyrics.

Children Of Autumn

One Day I heard a song that I knew,
It was simple and honest, and something rang true,
It was telling me of a place that I knew,
It was telling me of a tale that I knew,
It was magic and wonder all mixed in one,
It was moonbeams and sunbeams and hopes of the one,
It was telling me of a people who'd come long ago...

Chorus
Children of Autumn they were sent from above,
Smiling and Carefree they were laughing at me,
For I was crying and hoping
Someday, I'd be free,
Someday, I'd be me.

Verse 2
And now as I'm older, I walk all around,
And there is pain vast and sorrow,
And everyone frowns,
Yet there are questions with answers,
Yet we all seem so bound,
I also frown.

Chorus repeats

Bridge
And I begged them not to leave me this way,
But they laughed once again and started walking away.
As I saw them leave, I heard them say,
"The light in you had started to fade."

Chorus ends song

Now remember this song came to me two years before Julianne was born. Again I have to ask where did this come from and why? Who are these children the song sings of? Why does the song suggest they were a people from long ago? And why children of Autumn, not Spring, for example?

It's a very simple song, but what I have learned along the way is that it is coded. Why do I say that? Because of the response I have had every time I have sung it.

The first time I sang it, I received a standing ovation (much to my surprise). People flooded the stage with tear-streaked faces saying "Children of Autumn – Children of autism." Other times, people cried. Now, that could be down to my singing, of course, but I don't think so!

What does this simple song have to do with autism?

Dare I even put this to print… hmmm… And yet, I do believe what I am about to say, so here goes.

I believe that in some other dimension, at some other time, a group of beings got together. Many beings, many brilliant beings, who looked at our earth and said amongst themselves, "boy, these guys and gals are in trouble. Look at what they are doing to themselves; to their environment; to each other. Wow, they need some help!"

As a collective, they agreed that they would come to earth with the intention of helping us to raise our frequency, allowing us the chance to see and truly witness, once and for all, how powerful we are, how loving we can be, and how creative we can be.

As I said earlier, the label they received has been autism, but I think it should be AWE-'tis-'EM.

Now, I know I am going to lose some of you by saying this. "People? From another dimension? *Choosing* to have autism?" I can hear you already, and you are entitled to your beliefs, bless you.

I, too, am allowed to have my perceptions.

Part of why I have chosen to write this book is because I know that if you are reading this, you too may be having magical, mystical experiences; questioning your right-mindedness. I am telling you: you are NOT crazy. You have been selected because of your openness and willfulness. I want you to know that you are not alone anymore. The family of light I was alluding to earlier is growing. And right on time. Like I said before, "We're gonna start a revolution."

How did I come to this understanding?

Receiving the song seeded this idea. That was in 1994. Then I began to observe. When I look at all the parents who have sacrificed their careers, their financial dollars and their time to 'work-play' with their child, day after day. I am in awe.

Every parent today is believing, with every ounce of possibility, that their child can and will heal. And many children have emerged, and continue to emerge, from autism fully, miraculously healed. What is that doing for our planet? Imagine how much love is being created right now on this planet of ours, by all those people who are working in their special therapy room, with their unique child, right this minute.

And what is happening to the parents and all those thousands—perhaps millions—of volunteers and caregivers who interact with these children?

From my personal experience, you become more loving and, of course, that permeates into all your relationships. You become much more flexible.

So, do you think having people who are more flexible will be good for our planet? Please excuse my sarcasm!

You become much less judgemental, much more forgiving, and much more tolerant of differences. Your creativity expands. You are more outrageous, more focused, more present and more patient: all qualities that lead to a world full of much more love, more tolerance and thus peace.

You see what I mean? Couple this with a vast number of humans wanting organically grown food; pure, accessible water and less pollution, and programs start mushrooming everywhere, ultimately helping our Earth heal.

All because of autism.

I believe these children have a plan to be the instigators of love on this planet of ours. Why? Let's face it. Whether we like to admit it or not, there is a lot of corruption on our planet. And yes, we can try to band together and fight it, but doesn't that just keep us in the same frequency we've been in for so long? I for one, am leaving the fight (and have left it) by holding another belief: that by growing the love on our planet, we will ultimately leave the fight behind. The love will overcome the fight as a river overcomes the riverbank when it swells and expands.

That's my theory. And I know it's a bit out there, but it makes sense to me; so I'm sharing it with you.

I am so grateful to all these people with autism, who had such a trust in us that we would take the high road, so to speak, and sacrifice earthly things for a time, to grow the love. Thank you for believing we could change.

Chapter 2—Here And Now: What Do We Do Now?

Seven years old, non-verbal, not toilet trained and misdiagnosed. We were on the wrong path.

And then the first of many miracles occurred.

A friend of mine handed me a book titled *Happiness is a Choice, by Barry Neil Kaufman.*

"Have you ever heard of these people?" he asked me.

"No," was my simple response.

"I would check them out," he said.

So I did.

I read the entire book that night. I knew intuitively that these people were connected to something that could help my daughter. I phoned them the next day and spoke to a very lovely lady named Zoe, who convinced me that even though my daughter had not—at that time—been diagnosed with autism, coming to the Options Institute would be a tremendous step in the right direction for us all.

She was right. How we got to this beautiful place in the Berkshires, and what happened there, makes up this chapter.

Perhaps you have heard of the Son-Rise program?

The founders of this magnificent place had a child with autism way back in the day—1973 to be exact. They (like you and I) searched all over North America for the best program they could find for their young son. They were not at all impressed with what they found, so they started their own program. Guess who runs the Options Institute today? You guessed it. Raun Kaufman—the once severely autistic little boy—now runs the entire company! Fully recovered from autism, his story lays the groundwork for what the Options Institute does at the Autism Treatment Center of America.

When you arrive at the Options Institute, there is a plaque that reads "Where Miracles Happen". Miracles do indeed happen, and this place certainly knows the formula. At the end of my first week at this wonder-filled place, I felt hopeful for the first time that my beautiful child might one day speak, write, read, sing, hold my hand and tell me she loves me.

Originally, Julianne had a diagnosis of "mentally retarded". She was a seven-year-old girl who could not speak and was completely out of control. I use to call her Tiger, because she was so wild in her movements and behaviours: she would bite you, pull your hair, scream and throw tantrums. If you've ever watched the movie of Helen Keller's life, Jewels was very much like that. Between the feces smearing and all these other behaviours, I needed help. I found out that attending the Son-Rise program in Massachusetts, including my airfare and transfers, would cost me $5000: $5000 that I did not have! But somewhere inside me was this desire to go there. I knew deep down that somehow this place could help us. So, the magic began.

I needed to raise $5000. We held Improv nights; I wrote letters asking friends and family members to support our venture; we sold Valentines cookies. Dollar by dollar, the money came in.

Quite frankly, the outpouring of love and generosity we received made me cry.

It was an incredible experience to be in a situation where I had to ask my friends and family to give me money. When I was in high school and university, winning awards and scholarships left, right and center, I never dreamed I would one day become a sophisticated beggar. Of course, my ego wasn't too pleased with this new way of being, but it was my conviction of what I was doing that got me through it all. Asking for help was the only way to accomplish what I wanted to achieve, and I believed wholeheartedly in what I was out to accomplish: helping Julianne Shea to heal.

In the end, I think it was good for me to humble myself to such an extent. It was good for me to learn what it feels like to be on the other side of the fence; the lesser side; the needier side. It has certainly made me more compassionate to my fellow men and women. Today when I am asked to give, I am so happy to be able to support someone else's conviction. I embrace the Pay it Forward concept with all my heart, having been a recipient of so much love and generosity. So, with the $5000 in hand, off I went for a week of learning at The Place Where Miracles Happen.

I am most grateful to all the people who created this place and continue to nurture it. The first breakfast I had there, I sat beside a fellow who was known by his autistic students as White Bear. He was a lovely man from Texas and somehow the Children of Autumn song came up in our discussion.

"Oh well, you will have to sing it for us," he said.

I laughed. *Are you kidding?* I thought to myself. *I have never performed that song for anyone other than my children.*

How funny life is. For the previous five years, I had been performing a couple of one-person shows, and during the offseason, I had taught musical theater and voice. Before coming to the Institute, I had proclaimed that I would be on sabbatical for the next two years, ONLY working with Julianne. I had also affirmed that, upon returning from my trip to the Options Institute, I would not perform or teach for the next two years.

And yet here I was on my first morning before class, and a complete stranger is suggesting I launch the Children of Autumn song here.   He was very insistent, and so finally I agreed to sing it for him during a break from one of our classes. He became my unofficial agent for the song, and during every break after that he would escort me to someone at the Institute who he knew was a musician. Each person we spoke to liked the song but was unable to perform it with me.

White Bear had a plan that I would sing the song during our last class together as a group. As the week progressed, I learned many wonderful things. I was becoming more hopeful by the moment for my daughter and was introduced to the concept of Dialoging. (*Power Dialogues: The Ultimate System for Personal Change. Barry Neil Kaufman*). Overall, I was feeling more and more like myself again: lighter, freer and more joyous.   Friday arrived—the last day of our scheduled classes—and it was my birthday. That day, I would choose whether or not to sing the Children of Autumn song—by then eight years old—in public for the first time.

One of the learnings I acquired while I was at the Institute was never to do anything that I didn't genuinely want to do. This idea was repeated many times during the week: Don't go into a session with your 'special' child just because you feel like you should or you must. Only go into a session with your child because you want to.

I remember Samahria Lyte, one of the founders, quite clearly saying, "These kids are very happy where they are. You are the one who wants to change them. Do not be a martyr for them; it will only create resentment and unhappiness. Go into your sessions because you want to. There you will find your strength and joy." This concept, I was beginning to transfer to all areas of my life. The beautiful realization here, of course, was that I could no longer play the victim if I was always choosing what I wanted to do. That was a big learning for me; I had played the victim for many years.

During a break, I went for a walk, and I asked myself, "Do you want to perform the Children of Autumn song today?"

Sure, I was scared. My ego was worried about how it would be received; how it would sound acapella. After walking the beautiful property at the Options Institute, I found the answer coming out of me. Yes, I did want to sing it for my fellow participants. It was time to bring it to the public.

The song had been received eight years ago, and only Griffin, Julianne and Jeff had heard it. *Are you sure?* I asked myself.

Yes, came the response.

I went back to our classroom and gave White Bear the thumbs up; I was up for the challenge.

Well, the class—our last class together as a group—went overtime, and I was unable to give the song its inaugural performance. But now the desire to share was large in my body. It had grown. The song wanted to be heard. White Bear and I conferred and decided the only chance left to perform the song would be at the lunch hall during the lunch hour. There would be more people there than just our group, but it was the only chance we would have. I walked back to my room, contemplating all the way how much I now wanted to perform this song. I was still nervous, but there was a bigger force overriding the fear in me now.

Sometimes we just have to jump off that cliff, so to speak. Seize the moment, some would say. Grab it while you can.

It's as if something had been growing and maybe not consciously) for a very long time, and then suddenly, in a matter of 24 hours, its birthing time appeared.

I walked over to the lunch hall and stood myself in line to receive the fantastic food that had been prepared for us. Feeling a little queasy, I sat down with my new friends discussing the week we had all experienced and then made contact with White Bear.

"Are you ready?" he asked.

"Soon," I said.

I went to the bathroom, did a few warm-up exercises that I always do before a performance, and made my way back out to the front of the lunch hall. It was time. White Bear introduced me to everyone in the room and handed over the stage to me.

I love it when we override our fears. I love it when we push ourselves because we want to share something that we believe will, in some small way, help others. I love it when we trust ourselves enough that we will make it through this, no matter what happens. I love it when we choose love over fear.

So I began. I introduced everyone to how the song had 'come' to me, just as I explained the story to you earlier in this book. I took a breath, looked out at my audience and started to sing. I remember, very clearly, feeling as though I could see my daughter and my son; as if they were in the back of the room, somehow cheering me on and encouraging me to be as big and beautiful as I could be. The song ended, and the room rose to their feet with a standing ovation. I was quite shocked. Happy birthday to the Children of Autumn song and me. It was a day I will never forget. It was the beginning of many wonderful experiences. As the song says, "It was magic and wonder all mixed in one."

The next day, I boarded a plane returning home. I was very excited about starting to implement the ideas I had learned at the Options Institute with Julianne. Inspired, and ready to start the greatest adventure of my life. I felt revitalized. Time to get to work!

At this time, Julianne had been in a classroom setting with other children her age for the preceding two years. Frankly, she made minimal progress in that environment. Whenever I picked her up, she was either asleep or screaming or had a diaper full of poo or pee. When I dropped her off at school it was an equal nightmare: she screamed the whole way in.

Something needed to change. Julianne was deserving of an education. I still believed there was an intelligent being in there; we just needed to find the magical keys to let her out.

With the Options Institute experience behind me, I approached our school's principal asking for a small room where Julianne could work with an aide, one-on-one, in a distraction-free environment. I reported on what I had learned at the Institute and, given that Jewels had been in the public school system for two years now (with many behavioral problems resulting) they were willing, I think, to try anything. At the same time, there was an article on the success of the Options Institute and the program I had just participated in—the Son-Rise Program—in Macleans magazine that month, which certainly strengthened my case further. So we began. Kim Wallace, our first aide, met with me, and I explained the basics of the program to her. We set up a small playroom where we put a shelf up, out of Julianne's reach, where we had some toys, some books, and some puppets. Inside the playroom was a small camping toilet. Our goal was to encourage Julianne to speak. Within the first week of using this new approach, Julianne said one hundred new words. By the first month, she spoke one thousand words and was forming small sentences.

"I want the doll," she would say. "I want juice."

I was ecstatic. My daughter, who was seven years old, was able to speak. Oh, my God! Hallelujah! Let the miracles begin!

Kim and I were both excited. We added more goals to our list: to teach her how to count, to read the alphabet, to bead, to listen to her body to know when she had to use the toilet.

It took Julianne three months to learn to count from one to ten, but learn it she did. Using the Letterland program (a reading program from England) we introduced the alphabet. Using songs, poems, and as much outrageousness as we could muster, Julianne learned to read.

A further goal was to encourage loops: in Julianne's speech. In other words, if I say "Hi, How are you?" you might say "Fabulous, and you?" thus creating one loop. We used many puppets to encourage the realization of these goals and designed many games for us to attain success. We found out quickly that Julianne had a definite sense of humor, and she loved music and books. One of her first spoken words ever was, in fact, "book". We used her motivations wherever we could.

After a few weeks, I recruited another excellent teacher in Julianne's life, and then another and another. Everyone who came on board took to the Options Institute teachings—the Son-Rise program—immediately. My job grew into recruiting more volunteers, training all these people, and doing my hours with Jules.

From three of us, the team rather quickly increased to ten, which allowed us to do ten hours of one-on-one work with Julianne in her "special room". We had children working as volunteers (including her brother Griffin, which I have to say brought tears to my eyes), high school students, moms, dads; all bringing their love and desire to help every time they arrived. I once had a beautiful mom dress up as a doctor to work with Jules. I was observing Les this particular day (which I often did, to give the therapists feedback and ideas). I don't know who was the luckier one that day: Julianne, as she got to work with Les, or me, as I got to listen to her and was rolling over laughing so hard outside the room.

It was moments like this that made me believe some superior force was working with us and was on our side cheering us on to success. Always, even when I was down in my lowest emotions, someone or something would happen to bring me back up and continue with this work. This hour with Les as 'Dr. Les' was one of those many moments. It was such a testament of love, the real stuff: people going out there, using all their creative talents to help another being, and doing it for free. No dollars involved.

Wow, my heart cries tears of joy remembering it. I will ALWAYS be grateful for those gifts as they truly were the glue that kept me together. Thank you so much.

The first six months were INTENSE. It was an amazing time in my life. I was forever training people. I was holding and running a weekly meeting at my home for the Julianne Miracle in Motion Team. I myself was working with Julianne daily. We even designed a newsletter. And, of course, fundraising became part of my life.

I was busy, but life was full: my Julianne was finally learning.

Months passed, and Julianne continued to grow. Our list of goals continued to rotate. Some team members left to pursue other interests, new members joined. I was busy! After a year of working with Jules, I was inspired to return to the Options Institute a second time. Thanks to a wonderful friend, Jacinta Broemeling, our family received a grant of $5000 to cover all expenses required to make this dream a reality.

I remember when the call came from a lovely lady on the Eleanor Case board in Edmonton. "We had our annual general meeting last night, and we agreed unanimously to award this money to you so you could pursue your work with your daughter."

Well, by now you know I am a crybaby, so of course I cried… and then I screamed a big massive "YAHOO!!!!"

Miracles do happen. I was going to the Options Institute for the second time. My friend White Bear wasn't there this time. In fact, we had lost touch, probably because I was so busy with Julianne and keeping Griffin somewhat mothered, but I will always be grateful for his prodding and midwifery of the Children of Autumn song.

Kim Wallace, our friend and Jewels's school aide, came with me on this venture. We met many wonderful new friends from all over the world, all with high hopes for their child (and in some cases children).

As always, the Institute was a place of great sharing and nurturing. We learned more skills that would ultimately help Julianne grow: how to give better feedback for our team; more on the dialogue process; how to hold effective group meetings; how to keep the volunteers inspired; and, of course, we all received healing. This is one of the things about the Options Institute that I adore. They can create a space where there is so much love and trust on everyone's part—facilitators and participants alike—and great healings come about not only for the children who have autism, but also for their parents.

All through my life up to this point, I had put a lot of pressure on myself to be perfect. Where that push originally came from I do not know, but certainly I had a definite interpretation of what perfection meant to me, and often I wasn't meeting the mark (probably because it was too darn high).

I was in a perpetual state of feeling not good enough. There was always something not right: too fat, too many pimples, didn't get an A+ on a paper, not enough money, too much rust on my car, don't own a home yet and I'm how old? And on and on it went.

How the Options Institute managed to help me transform this idea, I can't remember—I guess you will have to go there yourself to find out! I do remember the moment I 'realized'—and I say it in quotations because a friend of mine plays with words a lot and points out that realized means to see with real eyes—that my perfection lies in my imperfection. Ha ha to you, ego! Got you at your own game! Touché!

I'm not even sure if I will be able to explain this in words, but in my body I had a realization that the way I am— here and now in every moment—is Perfect. It is what I am. With all my imperfections, I am perfect. I think the key words here are 'I am'. 'I am' is not 'I have a bachelor degree', or 'I own a mansion', or 'I am the fastest runner on the planet.' 'I am' is 'I am'. It is just an 'is-ness'. To my mind, it has nothing to do with what I do or accomplish or acquire. It is something that is always with me, and it is this piece that is the perfection.

Let me be as clear as I can in what I am saying: I am not in any way suggesting that anyone who hurts another person or our earth or even someone else's property is behaving perfectly. What I am saying is that separate and distinct from our behaviors is a being and that being (you, me and, yes, even the axe murderer) was created perfect. This is my belief. And it is just a belief.

Where we get all messed up is when we define who we are by what we do and how we behave, and often also by what we own. It seems that there are layers upon layers that need to be checked off before we can believe we are perfect. The switch that I made in my thinking while I was at the Institute was that I let go of the need for a checklist at all. I made a choice that the checklist was not serving me, so I threw it away. That, in turn, gave me space to just be; I gave myself space to relax and maybe even like myself as I was, at that moment. I remember throwing my arms into the air with a great sense of relief, and saying, "I lost! If there is a race that we are all in, I concede now. I lost."

From my experience, it seems that there is no way of actually attaining perfection until we embrace the imperfect in ourselves. The imperfections are the behaviors, the choices, the actions, the thoughts that we choose to have. I learned by interacting with Julianne in all her imperfections that she was perfect. As is. And as she grows, her perfection remains intact. And yes, of course, I cried as I realized this all… you are starting to know much about me.

The Options Institute is a place I encourage you to visit. Going to www.autismtreatment.org will take you to their website. They also have a YouTube channel you can subscribe to, called autism treatment. I recommend you watch "Autism Recovery Clip 1: Jade's Son-Rise Program". Many questions you have might be answered here. You are in good hands with these people. They are indeed bringing Heaven to Earth.

Chapter 3 — Expanding The Healing: Introducing Jonathan Alderson and IMTI

After my trip to Massachusetts and learning how to initially set up a home-based program, back in beautiful Jasper, Alberta, we quickly realized that even though we received in-depth direction to start sessions with Julianne, and we felt super 'pumped-up; we would need ongoing leadership and support. The mountains that surrounded us felt somehow protective and empowering, yet I acknowledged that we were remote, with only a few services in town. Now, what I needed was a like-minded professional to come to Jasper, to observe us in our home life and to train Julianne's team.

Once again, the user-friendly universe responded to my focused intention; I called the Autism Treatment Center of America to schedule a support visit, and what I got was even more than I imagined: our very own Superman!

Jonathan Alderson is the Founder and Director of the Intensive Multi-Treatment Intervention program for children with autism (www.IMTI.ca). He was on the Son-Rise Program Rolodex at the time I called for in-home support because he had trained and worked there for eight years. He knew the Son-Rise methods intimately, trained to their highest level as a senior family and therapist trainer, and had gone on to study and build upon this foundation to create a ground-breaking approach that combines a wide range of strategies in a way that I haven't come across in any other program. He is also the author of a must-read book, *Challenging the Myths of Autism.* Jonathan is certainly brilliant, with an undergraduate degree in developmental and educational psychology from Western University and a Masters from Harvard. It is his heart, however—his sincerest desire to help—that won all of us over.

They say like attracts like. Jonathan is by nature a playful and loving person. So, where better would a potential miracle-maker choose to do some training than an autism center that bases its approach on a non-judgemental attitude and play? Just before we met him, he was responsible for the autism Treatment Center's Son-Rise Program UK division, based in London, and working with families in Spain, Holland, Ireland and across England. He had worked with over two thousand families and their children on the spectrum. However, thankfully for us, he had repatriated to his home in Ontario, Canada with a vision to offer families all that he had learned plus a missing link: how to successfully combine all of the different therapies and strategies parents and professionals learn from the many sources they come across. We were jazzed about Son-Rise, but I knew there were several other important approaches I wanted to include in my daughter's programming and, like every parent I've ever talked to, I didn't know how to piece it all together. Jonathan had started to specialize in answering this very question!

Being courageous and brave (as all superheroes are) Jonathan made the trip to our mountain home. I remember picking him up from Edmonton one day when the temperature had dropped to -35 degrees Celsius! As we drove to Jasper, he asked if I had chains for the snow tires. "No, we're not that remote!" I said and smiled. Indeed, coming all the way from Toronto, into the blustery snow-capped province of the mountains, he showed his willingness and commitment to helping families like ours whenever he can.

During the first few hours of consultation with Jonathan, he explained two of the most important ideas behind a Multi-Treatment program: Order and Timing.

Jonathan's training was extensive: the play-based Son-Rise Program; behavioural science at university; courses in home-schooling, massage and remedial reading; introductory certificates in Brain Gym and HANDLE; and dozens of workshops and seminars on the biomedical treatment of autism, to name a few. Throughout all of this, Jonathan has asked two questions over and over. First, he tries to determine in what order all of the wide range of treatments, approaches, and strategies should be used to maximize their benefit to any individual child? Second, in what timing? In other words, when should you start the second strategy or program, and when should you end the first one? Should they overlap? Can two different approaches be used at the same time? Would this be confusing to a child, or would one treatment be a positive catalyst for another?

Jonathan's first trek to Jasper focused our team's work with Julianne immensely. He mapped out the different phases we would go through together, and introduced attitudinal tools to help us all maintain positivity throughout this experience. Alongside the one-to-one therapy he directed, he explained the importance of ensuring Julianne's physical health is up to par for all of the hard work, concentration, and learning we would ask her to do. Like a top athlete who trains their body for top performance, he taught us how learning is a biological process (the brain is a lump of fat, which is one reason why we need good fats in our diet, for example). So if we want to support Julianne's top cognitive performance we had to ensure her brain was getting the right nutrition and as few toxins as possible.

He taught us about the gut-brain-behaviour connection, distinguishing between physical heath symptoms and symptoms of autism. Then he introduced us to the SCD diet and the book *Breaking the Vicious Cycle* by Elaine Gottschall, B.A., M.Sc. The book is based on her life-long work to help people with Crohns, Celiac, and now individuals with autism, rid their gut of toxic yeast overgrowths. I turned my kitchen upside down (all for good, in the end).

After employing this diet for two weeks, we saw a definite increase in Julianne's eye contact, her ability and desire to interact with people, and her increased focus and calm. While Julianne was on this diet, she ate no sugar, no carbohydrates, and no processed food for two years. I learned to cook with unpasteurized honey and believe it or not Julianne's birthday cake was always such a hit that people would ask me for the recipe. When making a significant change such as diet in your life, you need to be patient with yourself and your child. Also, you need to trust that if your child accidentally eats something not on the diet you will all survive. "Do your best" is a mantra I started to employ early on in my journey. Let's face it; you have A LOT going on. I lived it; I understand the pressures.

My goal here is to inspire you to make the changes that will most serve you. Just like Jonathan inspired us. Making the dietary changes are worth the effort. I guarantee it. I know some people are afraid to take sugar away from their child such as pops, dessert items, ice cream, chocolate, and candies, but I promise you your child will be so much better off without these things. You can do it! From *A Course in Miracles*, a book I have been studying for many years, there is an affirmation that states, "There is nothing my Holiness cannot do." *Course in Miracles – Helen Schucman:* make this one of your mantras! Be kind to yourself as you make changes and trust in the decisions you make. Trusting yourself is an enormous part of this initiation to these changes.

Despite the bears, elk, and caribou, Jonathan visited us in Jasper many more times during the next four years. Jonathan successfully lobbied for continued support from the school for us. Meanwhile, Julianne began to do things we didn't think imaginable as Jonathan is brilliant at helping break down goals into tiny manageable steps. For example, when we were teaching Julianne how to jump forward, each step was carefully outlined, from foot positioning, to knee bending, to arm swinging, to lift off, to propelling forward, to landing. With great enthusiasm and excitement for four months, we inspired Julianne to jump into a hula-hoop lying on the floor. I can honestly tell you (because I remember it so vividly) that the first time Julianne jumped into the hoop it was as if she had won an Olympic gold medal. It was an incredible moment that came after months of repetition, and continual focus and visualization of her jumping, all the time finding inspiration in the micro steps forward and somehow trusting, believing she could do it, then the moment occurs. VICTORY!!! ACCOMPLISHMENT!! DREAMS MANIFESTING INTO REALITY! BLISS! After embracing her and spinning her around with great love, the next moment brought reality back to the room.

"Do it again," I prompted. "Jump into the hoop again Julianne."

A moment of disbelief entered the space. Fear surfaced. Had she actually learned it or was it just a fluke? Could she do it again? Fear reared its ugly old face once again.

"Come on Jewels you can do it!" I cheered.

Sure enough, she jumped into the hoop again and again and again. Another miracle to add to the list. Now, jumping over the edge of a hula-hoop laying flat on the floor may seem small to some, but this little accomplishment became the springboard for many of Julianne's physical achievements. Today she enjoys swimming, downhill skiing, cross-country skiing, long distance running, and yes, even bike riding on two wheels.

Nowadays when people tell me "You can't do that," I often don't say anything out loud but, inside, a fire has been lit, thanks to the gift of experiences I have witnessed from working with my beautiful daughter; and I quietly say to myself, "Yes you can!" I have watched the impossible dream become possible—like the caterpillar becoming the butterfly. With great patience, great focus and never ending will, I do believe great things can be accomplished. And what great joy accomplishment can bring.

Sometimes things can take a really long time to manifest, as in the case of teaching Julianne to recognize the numbers one to five symbolically. For two and a half years, this goal remained on our roster faithfully. We created all kinds of games around this aim. I remember giving Jewels horse rides on my back around the room with the numbers one to five strewn on the ground. When we arrived at one of the figures she had to tell us what the number was and then the horse went a little crazy, bucking her and moving her around from side to side. She seemed to love the game as she eagerly climbed on my back time and time again and giggled joyfully every time the "horsey" bucked her and swooshed her around. Sometimes she would get the right answer, sometimes not. Every time we would cheer her on with

"Good try... it's five... this is the number five" and then show her the number again. Two and a half years later, after days and days of testing, we knew Jewels finally had an understanding of these figures. Again, as above with the jumping exercise, so much Joy flooded in. Success! She did it; she knows the numbers. Yeah!!! Great joy and then again a moment of dread.

Oh my God, I remember thinking. *It's going to be another two and a half years to teach her the numbers six to ten!* Which triggers two important thoughts I would like to share with you.

First, in our case, this did not occur. What did occur was rather incredible. After spending two and a half years of every day working on the numbers one to five, a week into teaching Jewels the numbers six to ten she had them nailed. She had eleven to twenty a week later and so on— Add another like to the Miracle page. Incredible. So what had happened? My belief is that some groove was created into Julianne's brain by going through the process of repeating the one to five numbers for so long. When new information was being taught the 'highway' was being built. Two and a half years was no longer the time required to learn something new.

Julianne learning her numbers opened up a whole new level of experience for us all. Suddenly we could play games. We could start adding and subtracting. We could introduce money and how that works. We played many hours of Monopoly, Snakes and Ladders, card games and bingo. We made up games. A whole new world had been birthed. Often I would think, *What if we had quit? What if somewhere in there, between day one and day nine hundred and ten, we said, "Forget it. This is not working. She is never going to get this. Let's just give up."*

What a completely different reality we would have created for ourselves. Luckily, by some force, we didn't quit. Jonathan Alderson helped me maintain my inspiration during the challenging times using attitudinal tools that reconnected me to my love for Julianne and to my will. There were some trying times no doubt, particularly around toilet training. But, like in the number example, we persevered and were successful. Another incredible teaching in patience and persistence.

The second important thought turns around the possibility that teaching Jewels numbers six to ten could have taken her another two and a half years. If we can make the time to be with people we love and help them learn, does it matter how long the process takes? This is a big question that perhaps we all need to ask ourselves. Are we willing to teach people we love even if it takes a seemingly long time? One of the greatest lessons I learned was from Samahria Lyte Kaufman, co-founder of the Options Institute. I had a private session with her once in which she taught me NEVER to go into the playroom with Julianne unless I wanted to. As Jonathan himself had been fortunate enough to have been trained by her, he was a constant reminder to me of this wisdom.

What I have experienced in all the hours I played with my daughter is that when I was truly present and when I was truly Loving (therefore not controlling Julianne in any way or demanding anything from her), I was joyful. The fact that she was learning things kept me going for certain and was, of course, wonderful. My personal belief now is that if I have the time to teach something that I understand to someone I love, and they are open and willing to learn, I will exercise patience and persistence for as long as required. When we are in that loving place it's a feel-good for everyone, so how can anyone lose? In *A*

Course in Miracles, one of the teachings is "To give is to receive." From my experience with Julianne, I now believe this to be true. Again, it's one of the reasons why I think these beings came to us: so we could experience ourselves as that which we are— love beams.

Jonathan created six phases of program development, which the child works through. His specialty is in the order and timing. When we first met with him, we were in Phase 1: Free Play and Building Rapport and Relationship. Once a secure connection with Julianne had been made, and we knew she was now interested in interacting with us (even for short periods of time) we moved into Phase 2: Expanding Activity Repertoire.

Under Jonathan's direction, we used a set of charts called HELP (Hawaii Early Learning Profile) as a baseline of behavioural learning objectives. These charts outline what is normal/neurotypical development for children aged zero to six in several developmental domains, from language to fine motor and self-help skills for example. We identified two goals for each area of development. As Julianne accomplished a goal, we moved on to the next one. Jonathan assisted us in brainstorming activities and strategies to allow goals to be met as quickly as possible.

Eventually, we moved into Phase 3: Academic Curriculum and Table Work. During this phase, Julianne was willing and wanting to sit at a table and practice her printing, math skills and reading for longer periods of time. We had built her intrinsic motivation to learn, and we included rewards to keep her on track.

"Jewels", I would say, "We are going to read five pages of this book and then you can choose a song we can dance to."

On the ski hill, it sounded something like this, "Jewels, we are going to do five runs, and then you can have some fries."

Very clearly defined expectations as well as clear rewards.

Jonathan calls the fourth phase "Peers and Playdates". Jonathan taught our entire team the best protocol to work with when another child was over for a play date with Jewels. I remember once when a young girl named Zoe came to play with us in our playroom. The two girls got all dressed up in play clothes and enjoyed tea together. Each girl toted a large brimmed hat and a coloured feather boa. Julianne had a big smile on her face the size of an ocean.

A young boy named David was a regular in our playroom and possibly Julianne's first crush. The two of them played "bus" often with a large cardboard box, where David was the bus driver and would ask Julianne for her fare, where she was going, how her day was and so on. For two years, girls a few years older than Julianne from the high school would visit with her for twenty minutes daily. Whether it was Megan or Ashley, Julianne looked forward to that time. The two would play games, do artwork together, or simply have a conversation. Many sweet moments with these courageous children of the neighborhood who volunteered their time, shows there is hope for our planet.

Today Julianne loves deeply. Once when she was talking to her uncle on the telephone, I overheard her say " You know relationships are very important to me. I do them differently than other people do but they work for me." Certainly a true statement. As Julianne to this day will decide when, and if, she is going to interact with you. Rest assured though, if she does choose to engage she will undoubtedly contribute something appropriate, uplifting or thought-provoking.

Jonathan is a real gem. We accomplished a lot with him as our guide, and he helped us unveil many of Julianne's hidden talents. I honestly believe Julianne is capable of doing things today that she would not have been able had he not "flown" into our lives. We will forever be grateful for all the gifts he brought to our lives. Superheroes do exist, folks, as do miracles. You just have to ask for one and be open to receiving them.

Oh, and you have to believe you are entitled to them.

Today he is like family to us. Just writing his name brings a smile to my face and a warmth in my heart. We have skied with him, jogged five km together around Lac Beauvert, visited the ROM in Toronto, celebrated birthdays, and will undoubtedly continue to soar with him.

On a visit to Saint Baume, France, we found ourselves in the very sacred cave where it is said Mary Magdalene lived for twenty years after Jesus ascended. Julianne—in a very peaceful state—channelled some thoughts of how important forgiveness is for our planet. Following this material she had channelled out of the blue, she looked at me and quietly said, "Jonathan Alderson."

I was a bit surprised that Jonathan was on her mind in this cave, because it was so random and at that point we hadn't seen him in a few years. An excellent example of how impressions last. Julianne, I believe, knows all the love this man brings to his work. He is indeed a blessing to our Earth and a Superhero for our children.

I encourage you to do everything in your power to acquire this man's services. Remember "There is nothing your holiness cannot do."[3] To reach Jonathan, please visit his website at www.imti.ca or www.JAlderson.com.

---

[3] *Course in Miracles*, Helen Schucman

Chapter 4—Healing The Gut

One of the great discoveries I made on this journey was how important the gut was—and is—in autism. Indeed it is important for everyone, but for Jewels and others on the spectrum it is critical.

And so, in this chapter, I want to look at three aspects of gut health.

First, I'll continue the discussion of diet that I started in the previous chapter.

Second, I'll look at Hyperbaric Oxygen Treatment.

Lastly, I will explore probiotics and some cutting edge therapies that have entered the playing field regarding helping gut health.

The alternative health community is now convinced that the gut is our second brain. Healthy gut = healthy brain. Certainly embarking on any of these recommendations will be trying, as they sometimes require significant changes to occur. Big changes are sometimes uncomfortable. But, miracles are possible and exist, for everyone. You just gotta believe.

Diet

When Julianne was six months old, she was constipated. At six weeks old her liver was off. How do I know this? Fortunately for us, we were seeing a wonderful naturopath who worked out of Cobourg, Ontario. On our first visit after Julianne's perfect birth Hania, our doctor, noticed Julianne's liver wasn't working at full capacity (later, we would find out this is very common with people on the autism spectrum). She prescribed a homeopathic remedy for this. When I explained that I noticed Julianne was constipated, she showed me how to do baby belly massages, which helped a little, but this condition would become a constant in Julianne's life and a challenge for us all.

Before we knew that Julianne was on the spectrum, she ate a diet after the one-year mark typical of most children: pasta, Cheerios, sandwiches, cereals.

Carbs, carbs and more carbs!

And of course, she had the occasional sweet (her grandmother—my mother—loved sweets). Carbs and sugar for Julianne were a diet disaster, but of course, we were unaware of this at the time. Her constipation got worse instead of better and for years, on a regular basis, she would go for three days without a bowel movement. Then… well, you can imagine. It was a constant, never-ending loop, frustrating for everyone and I'm sure the initial cause of the feces smearing.

When Jonathan (Superman) Alderson came on board, he introduced us to the SCD diet, Elaine Gottschall's life's work. After two weeks on the diet, EVERYONE noticed a difference, not only in Julianne's bowel movements but—equally impressive—in her eye contact and willingness to cooperate with others. As discussed in the previous chapter, Julianne was on this diet for two years.

Hyperbaric Oxygen Treatment

A few years later, on a holiday to Puerto Vallarta, I serendipitously opened up a Mexican newspaper to an article on an autism clinic in Puerto Vallarta. I was blown away and had to check it out. They even had a Hyperbaric Chamber, which I had been introduced to by our then DAN (Defeat Autism Now) doctor, Dr. Bruce Hoffman. I received a tour upon my arrival and was just about to leave when who should arrive but the lady herself: the one and only Kerri Rivera. Immediately, she began to ask me what I was doing with my daughter and what her clinic could do for me. She handed me her card, smiled her beautiful smile, and left.

Three months later, a little snowflake entered my brain one Saturday morning with the word Mexico on it. *What? I thought to myself. How am I supposed to get to Mexico?* I was, by that point, a single mom. I laughed at how ridiculous my brain can sometimes be.

Just for kicks, I phoned Kerri to find out the cost of Hyperbaric Oxygen Treatment Therapy. I remember her specifically saying, "Just come. I want your daughter to experience this. If you can cover the cost of the oxygen, that would be great." She explained those costs to me. I now had a rough idea of what this venture would cost. I laughed again and got ready to go to the hockey arena. It was my turn to be the penalty box keeper for my son's hockey game. As I was standing on the ice, two different people that day came down to where I stood and put money in my hand. "For Julianne," they said. I was stunned. Then miracle of all miracles, I won the 50/50 draw (very unusual for me).

As I realized I had the winning numbers, that little voice in my head once again spoke. This time, it said *For Mexico.* Someone was leading me to Mexico, so of course we went. Three times, in fact, Julianne and I went back to Mexico for HBOT (short for "Hyperbaric Oxygen Therapy").

Hyperbaric chambers. Football players, hockey players and movie stars use them. Scuba divers who get into trouble have their lives saved by them. What are Hyperbaric Chambers? How are they useful to a person with autism? The first pressurized room used to treat health problems was built by an Englishman named Henshaw in 1662. However, it was not until over a century later in 1788, that compressed hyperbaric air was put to large-scale use in a diving bell for underwater industrial repairs of an English bridge.

If you're interested in the history of Hyperbaric Oxygen Therapy HBOT Hyperbaric, take a look at this article by the Richmond Hyperbaric Health Center:

http://www.richmond-hyperbaric.com/history-and-types-of-hyperbaric-chambers.html

HBOT is great, and I will share with you what I know of this modality. Timing is everything, and with HBOT, there is a best time to embark on this therapy. Kerrick Rivera is a mother to a child on the spectrum, advocate and writer. She has written a book entitled *Healing the Symptoms Known as Autism.* This material is controversial, but after living with this family for months, I know that Kerri and her family are 100% committed to helping as many children with autism as possible. Would I recommend this protocol to you? Yes. Will you face resistance from members of your family, friends, and medical team? You might. This is where you will have to listen to your inner voice, and I know sometimes that can be difficult.

Part of this initiation, as I've said before, will be to learn to trust yourself and your voice. What I *can* tell you about the people behind this protocol is that they are 100% genuine and intelligent. They are here to help in every way they can. They are willing to take the bad press and continue with the message. They are using this protocol on their child and gleaning fantastic results. When they were first being introduced to this protocol, Kerri's husband played guinea pig for the family. These are real people. Righteous people. People deserving to be believed. Many people have fantastic results with this program. I have used this protocol with my daughter. When she was on this program, her gut was at its optimal health.

Hyperbaric Oxygen Therapy brings down Inflammation

I remember the day I was in Dr. Bruce Hoffman's office, and he said, "You know your daughter's brain is on fire." Of course, at the time, I had no idea what he meant, but I do now.

Many of our children suffer from inflammation. A big reason for this is because of their unhealthy gut health. Address this by changing their diet and employing a protocol such as the one Kerri outlines in her book. Once you have addressed this issue, you can apply the use of a chamber for restoration to occur. Did you know that Hyperbaric oxygen actually creates new stem cells? The reason athletes and movie stars use these machines is because healing occurs that much faster. There are numerous videos on YouTube one can watch explaining the benefits of HBOT. An excellent read on this subject (and yes, I know you're busy but it is worth it) is *The Oxygen Revolution: Hyperbaric Oxygen Therapy* by Dr. Paul Harch. If I could download it into your brain, I would. What I can tell you is that this is a potent therapy and I encourage you to use it.

Probiotics

One thing you will learn rather quickly is that for every single person who says something is good for your child, there will be someone else who will tell you it is not. Again let me re-emphasize: this is where you need to develop a way of determining for yourself what is truth.

In their book *Brain Maker*, David Perlmutter, MD and Kristin Loberg strongly recommend that you add a probiotic to your child's diet.   Dr. Perlmutter, a neurologist, has been studying the gut-brain connection for many years.   According to Dr. Perlmutter and Dr. MacFabe from London, Ontario, Canada, "The science is clear that both diet and exercise are critical to our brain health." Based on scientific analysis "gut bacteria can tinker with your brain". I recommend you watch Dr. Perlmutter on Youtube, as well as Dr. Derrick MacFabe.

Dr. Perlmutter recommends foods that are fermented as a good source of probiotic. These include the Kombucha drink, sauerkraut, kefir, kimchi, and yogurt for those children who can digest dairy. If supplementing with a pill, he recommends you look for a product with Lactobacillus Plantarum, and a strain from the Bifido group with at least ten, twenty or fifty billion CFUs per capsule. He suggests you take your probiotic on an empty stomach and not with chlorinated water. Personally, I resonate with both these gentlemen and look forward to their future work. But that's just me. You need to make your decisions based on what resonates with you.

Another Medical doctor affiliated with autism, Dr.Tim Buie, also speaks on the subject of probiotics on Youtube, but he recommends that you *not* supplement your child with probiotics.

Welcome to the world of being a parent of a child with autism!

How do you decide what to do? Again that is your journey. Personally, I undertake as much research as I can, and then ultimately I let my gut—no pun intended—decide. I have made choices many people disagreed with, but I had the authority to make the decision and I did. There is only one thing I wouldn't do again, and I'll share this story later in Chapter 8.

Trust yourself. Your child does: that's why they are with you.

New Advances

Fecal transplantation (or Bacteriotherapy) is the transfer of stool from a healthy donor into the gastrointestinal tract of another. "At this time, the FDA has not approved Fecal Transplant, so it is still an emerging field," says Dr. David Perlmutter, "although we have seen intriguing results amongst people with autism so far." I recommend you keep a watch on this therapy. *The Autism Enigma* is a documentary I recommend you watch. Stay tuned. Once again, we return to the shit. This time, however, it may be the sweetest solution for our kids. Spirals abound!

Chapter 5—Attitudinal Tools: How To Empower Yourself

You have probably noticed that I speak a lot about miracles. I talk about them because I have witnessed many of them in my life. Experience, in my map of the world, equals philosophy.

Growing up in a Christian family, I certainly heard the word "miracle" mentioned a few times but didn't understand it then. Later, in my teens, I started to have some "dis-ease" with some of the doctrines I had been taught. Not everything I had been told was resonating with me. I began to push away from my upbringing and seek out what I felt and thought to be the truth.

First, I had to find a way to determine truth for myself. I started to read a lot of different works. I was open to exploring different types of religions. I participated in a Mystery School. I took sound healing courses and studied various healing modalities.

There is an array of modalities and ideas on our planet right now. What helped me "row my boat" through the fifteen years of growth with Jewels are the tools I am sharing with you. How I found *A Course in Miracles* (a text and study guide) is a miracle in itself.

The Course has been and is used by many people today: the wonder-filled Wayne Dyer and Doreen Virtue both say they have read the Course and applaud it. Marianne Williamson and Gary Renard have made careers around interpreting this fantastic book. There are study groups all over the world using this material. It is, in my humble opinion, divinely inspired and a GREAT tool to help you face any dilemma. I still (and probably always will) use many of the ideas this book shared with me.

In this chapter, I explore this text and how it can keep you attitudinally fit as you walk this path with your person who has autism.

The Options Institute taught me another tool that I also continue to use, called the Dialogue Process. In this chapter, I will also look at this process and how it can help you and explain to you where and how you can learn how to use this tool.

Next, I will introduce you to one of my favourite techniques, Spiritual Response Therapy (SRT). SRT is a very powerful way to clear old programs that you are holding and no longer serve you. "Like what?" you might ask. Self-punishment programs, conflict programs, and trauma programs, to name a few. I will share much about this modality in this chapter.

Finally, a technique I had started with my son Griffin back when he was two was infused with more depth through our time with Jonathan Alderson. *The Grateful Game* is a very simple game you can play alone, with five hundred people, in a bank line up, on an airplane, out loud, on paper— ANYWHERE—and the results are astounding. You just have to do it. My goal is to keep you in the game (so to speak) on the autism merry go round. Sometimes you're up and sometimes you're down. Any and all of these tools can and will help you go back up if you find yourself on a down. No need to judge the down. It is simply that. By applying any one of these techniques, you will quickly rise and be that much more present for you and your child. Back in the game, recharged and energized. Now that's just a whole lot of good!!

A Course in Miracles

Written by Dr. Helen Schucman, *A Course in Miracles* literally walked into my life. I was working part time at a supplement shop in Toronto when a woman returned this book to the store. As I held the book in my hands, I mused over the title. *A Course in Miracles*. Interesting, I thought. I opened it up and read a few words. My first impression was, "too religious for me".

I closed the book and went back to my duties. A few days later my wasbund and I were having some difficulties. I was quite upset as I started my shift at the store. A customer required that I go upstairs to the second floor of our building. As I was looking after her needs, I spotted the book *A Course in Miracles* in the mailbox of one of our staff members. I pulled it out, opened it again and read. This time, the words spoke to me personally. As if God Him or Herself opened the book and said, "Read this Grace, it will help you." I overlooked the overly religious over-tones. I knew I needed to have this book in my life so I ordered myself a copy. Upon receiving it, I started the Course.

I worked with this book intensely for over a year. When I moved to Jasper, it came with me. When I was performing, I would read a piece of it before every show. When I was working with Julianne, I practiced what I had been learning. To this day, I employ many of the tools it teaches.

The book is divided into three parts: A manuscript, a course, and a teacher's manual. The Course itself is made up of a different daily meditation. Each day you learn to see the world with new eyes. As you work through the Course, building on each lesson, you become masterful at seeing the world and yourself with much more ease and grace. As with anything the more you practice the ideas the course puts forward, the easier miracles occur for you.

A large part of the Course is learning how to forgive. With Julianne in my life, I had constant opportunity to practice forgiveness. In fact, I call her my forgiveness strengthener. Forgiveness as the Course points out "offers me everything I want." Ultimately I consider myself somewhat of a selfish person. What I mean here is, I enjoy feeling happy, peaceful and calm and I will do whatever is required for me to remain in these states as much as possible. By being a student of the Course, I have reaped the rewards of its teachings many times over. Still a mainstay in my library, I refer to it often.

Power Dialogues

I was introduced to *Power Dialogues* whilst at the Options Institute in Massachusetts. Written by Barry Neil Kaufman, one of the co-founders of the Institute, this was a tool I frequently used.

When I was seventeen years old, I experienced the phenomena of automatic writing. One piece of writing I still have, contains this piece of advice: "Pick your tools wisely and you will survive, I promise."

Choosing the Dialogue as a tool was a wise choice. Ultimately, the Dialogue is a judgment-free way of shedding light on beliefs you hold and then changing the ones you no longer like. Most of us operate like computers, meaning we have all these beliefs stored in our consciousness—many in our subconscious—that we wake up with each morning and again agree to. We go through our days repeating the same painful emotions over and over again because we haven't deleted or modified beliefs we acquired, sometimes decades ago. My beautiful Julianne was a master at pushing my emotional buttons and made me examine what beliefs I was holding onto which were not serving me.

Over the course of the past thirteen years, I would guess I have worked through a thousand dialogues, some at the Institute but many on my own. Every time I did one, I would be confounded that I even believed the beliefs I believed! Crazy but true. The Dialogue offers you an opportunity to change your beliefs into ones you want to live by. It allows you to become the author of your own life. It brings freedom.

As the Children of Autumn song says, "There are questions with answers, yet we all seem so bound." The Dialogue process helps you loosen the chains that have been binding you. It allows you to answer the questions you are asking, from an authentic place within you and by you.

To experience this process, you can contact the Options Institute at 1 (413) 229-2100. You can learn this process by attending the Options Institute or by purchasing the book: *Power Dialogues: The Ultimate System for Personal Change* by Barry Neil Kaufman.

SRT-Spiritual Response Therapy

In 2013, on July 22, at a Magdalene Feast Day event, Julianne spoke in such a way that an entire room stopped in its tracks, turned around and leaned forward to hear what she had to say. I remember wondering, as her mom, if I should stop her. Then, that wonderful thought-voice kicked in again saying, *No way. Let her rip!*

She was talking about programs. "Programs," she said, "that you keep running and no longer serve you."

"You have to let go of the programs," she said, "and replace them. You have to reach a point where you say enough is enough and make a change!"

We were all amazed at the message coming out of Julianne. It was said with such authority.

Nine months later I found myself in Sedona, Arizona, driving a new friend to an SRT session I had arranged for her. SRT stands for Spiritual Response Therapy. I dropped off my lovely new friend and drove around Sedona. My voice told me then, *You are going to bring Susan* (the woman doing the session on my friend) *to Canada. You are going to set this up. You and many others are going to learn SRT.*

OKIE DOKIE! I thought. But yes, you guessed it, we did just this, and in September 2014, sixteen women ventured to western Canada to learn this marvellous technique.

On day one, Susan spoke about the "programs" we were going to clear.

Chills ran up and down my body. Flashback to Magdalene Feast Day.

I knew instantly this is what Julianne was talking about.

SRT was started in 1988 by Robert Detzler. It grew out of a psychological therapy called Response Therapy which was created by Dr. Clark Cameron and his wife in 1985. Cameron was introduced to the core idea behind this therapy by Davis Cheek and Leslie Le Cron, who point out in their book, *Clinical Hypnotherapy*, that an ideomotor response is extremely valuable for locating hidden messages that cause problems in daily life.[4]

Let me explain. An ideomotor response is a physical signal, such as a finger lift or eye movement, made by the subconscious mind in response to a direct question, which bypasses the conscious mind. In the book *Techniques of Hypnotherapy*, Le Cron specifically identifies the pendulum as a tool that may be used to get an the ideomotor response without hypnosis. Using a pendulum and a set of charts designed by Robert Detzler, programs such as conflict, self-punishment, discarnate and trauma programs can be cleared. Sometimes the therapist needs to do research in order to clear the program(s) and then accesses the client's Akashic Records to deduce where the program had its beginnings. For some of you reading this, you might find the whole idea too bizarre. Parallel lives, past lives, and even future lives are some of the places where the therapist might be led when doing SRT. SRT also offers a number of healing charts, and a therapist will be guided there if a client requires healing.

For more information on SRT, please visit my website at www.childrenofautumn.com or the Spiritual Response Association (SRA) at www.spiritualresponse.com. The SRA "envisions a world where anyone can realize his or her full potential." On their website they state "Once an individual is clear about their vision, and past obstacles have been removed, it is easier to manifest the greater good." The way I see it, the more peaceful, contented people we have on Earth, the better for us all.

---

[4] https://www.spiritualresponse.com/about/history

The Grateful Game

When my son Griffin was two years old, his Uncle David was very sick and eventually passed on All Saints Day, November 1st. I remember the Halloween pumpkins vividly, as the candles burned into the morning hours. The nine months leading up to his passing were very challenging for all of us. We needed something to keep our spirits raised. One day driving in our black K car with red interior—our very own Chitty Chitty Bang Bang—we started to sing things we were grateful for.

"I am grateful for my voice," I sang.

"And I am grateful for my Dad," sang Griffin.

"I am grateful for our car," said I.

"And I am grateful for candy," said Grif.

And back and forth we went.

We found that even in the middle of this challenging situation we could find many things we were thankful for. What we noticed was how this little sing-song made us feel. Happy, contented, more peaceful. Did we feel guilty for feeling happy when someone we loved dearly was suffering? Because of my work with *A Course in Miracles*, I wouldn't allow that. "Guiltlessness created me guiltless," is one of the meditations a student of the course works with. Guilt is one of those emotions, like fear, that keeps us in a low vibration.

From my experience, the less I align with both of these feelings, the more helpful I can be. In other words, the greater the amount of happiness I can maintain in my body, the better it is for the whole world. I am of greater service to people when I am strong. I feel secure when I feel joyful and peaceful. From my life's journey, when I give in to guilt and fear, worry, and even sadness and anger, I weaken my spirit. For the most part, I don't beat myself up. If I do beat myself up on the odd occasion, it is because—like all of us—I too, am learning.

Exercising Gratitude is so simple: I can do it anywhere, it's free, and most importantly it works. Whenever I choose Gratitude, I rise into the states of joy, and I feel reenergized. When Jonathan Alderson came on board with us, he expanded our game to asking "Why?" after each thing we mentioned. Sometimes we would write down our answers, and often we would get Jewels to play secretary.

Why am I grateful for life? Because it gives me an opportunity to experience so many possibilities. Why am I grateful for my daughter? Because she has stretched me, like no other human on this earth has, to grow into the most loving, compassionate, will-full, creative person I can be.

Why am I grateful for you? Because my hope is that by reading this material you grow the light within you. The more light we have here, the less dark there is in the world.

Chapter 6–Family Of Light: Here To Help Our Earth

Chapter One told the story of how the then three-year-old Julianne led me to the book *Family of Light: Pleiadian Tales and Lessons in Living* by Barbara Marciniak.

Years later, after finding out Julianne's diagnosis of autism, my biological family had a difficult time with the demands of this disorder. The emotional and physical support I needed, they could not accommodate. The miracle (there is that word again) that did occur was that a group of people started to form around us—strangers really—that today I would call our Family of Light. People who would, and did, drop everything to help us when the need was there. Individuals who offered their time, their resources, their love. How I learnt to forgive my blood family form a part of this chapter.

Forgiveness is a mandatory part of the initiation into the frequency of the world of Awe-tism. I have often said that Julianne is my forgiveness strengthener. With her in my life, I was given lots to practice on. Why is forgiveness important? I believe the more easily we can forgive others, the easier it becomes to forgive ourselves. Often I have found forgiving myself is even harder than forgiving someone else. When we can truly forgive ourselves, we can heal. Once we do that, we can begin to heal others and our Earth.

It has been said that people with autism are like the canaries in coalmines, telling us that our water needs help, our food needs help, our animals need help, our air needs help. Their bodies reject these items or respond violently to them. Much forgiveness is required, and then, of course, action needs to be taken. Being around Julianne has influenced how I think about everything: the car I drive; the food I buy and where I buy it; the water I drink and where it comes from. Our Family of Light has expanded to include everything from the farmer from whom we get our eggs to the mountainside from where we get our water. How to work in balance is a lesson many of us need to learn; being with autism has at least started me on this journey, and it may also start you on yours.

I have cried many tears in the last twenty years. Some of joy, and, many of anger, hurt, and pain. I had moments where I felt like I couldn't go on anymore. I would sit in the corner of the playroom in the dark, with one light lit above me, slumped over... sometimes it felt like hours, sometimes it felt like days. I wanted this whole dream to end. I wanted a typical life. When I was swimming lengths in the pool, I would cry. I would cry in my car, in my room, in my kitchen, into my pillow. I would cry and scream at God. I cried a lot. So I want you to know that even though I do believe these kids are here on purpose, I understand the challenges of being a parent of a child with autism.

Why was I crying? For many reasons .

I feared for my daughter, for myself, and for my son. Fear ruled my life. There was a great amount of fear of being rejected by my friends, family and the society I lived in, because I wasn't seemingly measuring up. I didn't have a new car, I didn't own a home, I didn't have much money at all. Much of my fear came out of the societal conditioning that I believe has been instilled in us all: because I chose to "sacrifice" my career and work to be primarily with my daughter, my family's financial situation was far from healthy.

I was convinced, however, that I had to help my daughter and for whatever reasons I was committed to this goal. Almost twenty years have passed, and I am still here. During that time, I've learnt many things, some of which I'd like to share with you now in the hope that they may help you.

- We really don't need as much, materially, as we think we do to experience happiness.
- Worrying about what other people think of you is <u>STUPID</u>, so stop it.
- My friends are my friends (and you know who you are); God bless them all. They love me because of who I truly am, and not what I have or don't have.
- The Universe can provide for us (even materially) in ways we never would have imagined.
- If I lower my ego, I can make a beautiful home for my family so long as I believe I can. Living in North America, we are truly blessed at how many second-hand stores we have access to, where beautiful treasures can be found very inexpensively.

❦ Practising Gratitude on a daily basis continues to have a positive psychological impact on me that can be felt in many ways.

❦ I can only control myself, and it's all I am responsible for. I can offer advice, guidance, healing and inspire people to strive to be the best they can be but, at the end of the day, it is up to them how they live their life. Their choices are theirs, and mine are mine. Learning to let people live their lives the way they want to was a big lesson for me. Julianne, again, was an enormous teacher here.

❦ Acceptance of what IS makes for a happier me; it doesn't mean I can't aim for something else to occur, but both concepts can co-exist. I know it's possible to be happy in the present moment whilst still having dreams of what can be in the future. The key is to be grateful for what I have now, in the present moment, while at the same time, striving for what it is that I want in the future. I have learned that real patience, persistence, and focus is required in order for manifestation to occur.

❦ Investing in myself is a worthwhile practice. I have studied many modalities over the years, always with Julianne as the motivating factor. I have studied Reiki, Carl Ferrini's NOT technique, EMF Balancing, EFT, SRT and have been a client of Body Talks, Access Bars, Ortho-Bionomy, Osteopathy, Acupuncture, Homeopathy and Naturopathy. Every practice has offered us something. I recommend you use your instincts here and let your spirit guide you as to what to try.

❦ "Forgiveness offers me everything I want." (*A Course in Miracles* by Helen Schucman).

Practising this mantra has enabled me to regain balance within myself, many times.

When I first started our program with Jules, I lobbied for volunteers to join us. Children, teenagers, and adults stepped up to the plate—people that I didn't even know at that time. Many of these people have become like family to us, and we all learned beautiful things along the way. Each of us is amazed at how much Julianne has learned and continues to learn, since those early years. Being blessed with so many helpful people around us for so many years made it easier for me to forgive my biological family for not being able to provide support.

The Options Institute teaches that, "People are doing the best they can with the beliefs that they have." *A Course in Miracles* teaches specific exercises you can perform, when you feel the need to forgive someone. I practiced these ideas and found they did reap rewards. I also pondered the situation from my "map of the world".

Having studied and taught Drama for many years, I was able to look objectively at the key characters in my life as simply that—characters. I came to a place in my thinking where I decided for the sake of MY wellbeing that I was simply not going to allow two or three characters in my life story to upset me. As there were so many helpful, kind, generous people actively participating in our "play", I chose to exercise gratitude for their choice to be part of our team as opposed to spending energy on the two or three players who were supposed to be supportive and for whatever reasons couldn't be.

This ideology helped me a great deal. I was able to stay in my heart zone. Staying *up* was crucial for me to continue my work with my daughter. My number one priority was to help my children become the most independent, happy people they could be. <u>No one</u> was going to stop me from doing that, and no one did.

We have all heard the concept of Oneness, whereby we are all connected. Iris Schrijver, co-writer of *Living with the Stars: How the Human Body is Connected to the Life Cycles of the Earth, the Planets, and the Stars*, shares "Our bodies are made of remnants of stars and massive explosions in the galaxies. All the material in our bodies originates with that residual stardust, and it finds its way into plants and from there into the nutrients that we need for everything we do: think, move, grow." Being connected, we can be influenced by what the majority of people think and believe.

Ken Wilber, an American writer on transpersonal psychology, outlines four quadrants that affect our overall wellbeing. In quadrants three and four it is primarily our "family" affecting us: our immediate family, biological family, and then the family of our country or state and Earth. From my experience with autism in the house, all of these "families" may challenge you. My suggestion is that you connect yourself with people you resonate strongly with. Again, it's a question of trusting your instinct and being flexible, as it may turn out that they aren't who you thought they'd be.

I found it necessary to have support. Although I was still challenged by many members of my "family" (including Government), because I had such a deep level of emotional support I could and did weather every storm that hit my front step. Having this group of "uplifters" is why I am here today, writing this book. There were hundreds of people who supported us; they know who they are.

There was a core team that lifted me up every time I needed lifting and came when the call was put out. In 2009, I received a song on the Marmot ski hill, as Jewels and I were swooshing down, called *Couldn't Have Made It Without You.* It became part of a musical I co-wrote with Greg Deagle and SteV ChaShar. The musical is called — you guessed it—*Children of Autumn: A Musical Journey Embracing Evolution.* It is dedicated to our children, Our Children of Autumn. You can watch our first production on YouTube, on the Dave Baker channel.

Want to put on an autism-themed musical as a fundraiser for your own program? To find out how you can get your own copy of Children of Autumn, visit http://childrenofautumn.com/contact-us/

According to *The Path of the Spiritual Sun* by Belsebuub and Angela Pritchard, the Autumn is a mysterious time. "It marks an essential passage in the process of enlightenment that is often overlooked, misunderstood, and mistaken as dark and heretical. It is the time of balance between day and night before night takes over and brings the coming winter, a time of darkness and death. This duality between light and dark exists within humanity, and in the work of spiritual transformation. All things must die before they can be born, all spiritual ascent requires descent first, and all those who long for light must firstly face their own inner darkness and overcome it." This writing most certainly resonates with the past twenty years I just experienced. All of this alchemical work, my friends, is much easier to handle when you have a family of light around you. Everyone has one, and I encourage you to find yours.

Chapter 7–Fun(d)raising Techniques

Money, money, money.

Everything costs money: tests, vitamins, therapists, books, conventions, special toys, etc.

And how do you get money when you are busy running a program, and keeping yourself attitudinally fit and abreast of everything that is going on in the field of autism? You have to make time for it; YOU MUST. And you have to make sure you put the *fun* in your fundraising because the time you will be spending away from your program for this <u>must</u> be fun, otherwise *don't even bother*!!!

There are a million different ways to raise funds for anything you want to try with your child. One vital requirement (at least this was true in my case) is that you must become comfortable with asking for money. You must have conviction in the reason you are doing this in the first place. Write down your reasons and stick them up somewhere you'll see them, if you have to remind yourself.

One of the fundraising activities I undertook for some years was a newsletter we created. It asked for help for specific things, such as thirty Hyperbaric Treatment sessions, or a genetic test to be carried out, or to bring Jonathan Alderson to Jasper for five days. It updated everyone as to the gains Julianne had made in the past year and the new goals we had for the upcoming year. We included pictures and some writings from people on our team. Lastly, our local print shop, Tekarra Color Lab, always donated the printing of the newsletters, for which I am forever grateful.

To get 3 sample issues of our newsletter to inspire your own, visit
http://childrenofautumn.com/book-resources/

Asking for anything—especially money—isn't always easy. My ego had a tough time with this whole experience. I felt embarrassed and disappointed with myself and my abilities (or lack of them). At times I was angry that I even had to do this. This was NOT the way my life was supposed to go. Every year, what gave me the drive to fundraise was my conviction in what I was doing. There was just no other way to keep running the program I was running (which was yielding results), and maintain fulltime employment. Julianne's Miracle in Motion program was a 100% fulltime job.

The first time I asked for help was the hardest, and of course, Spirit played with some of the results just to test my convictions. I was scared: what would my friends think of me? Would I lose friendships over this? I remember going through my list of contacts: *should I send this person a newsletter?*

Eventually, I took the plunge and sent them all out, held my breath and waited. After about a week, results—little envelopes full of good wishes and cheques filled—my post office box. OH MY GOD… What a relief, and so many tears of gratitude. I felt so much love as a result of asking for this help. It really was an incredible experience. People astounded me with their generosity. *A Course in Miracles* says, "There is nothing to Fear; God is with me wherever I go." Indeed, I have learned this to be true.

We held many other fun(d)raisers over the years, selling Valentines cookies, organizing music benefits and Improv nights. We had groups running marathons for us, riding bicycles for us. We held bottle drives. We raised money through organizations such as the Lions Club, Ladies of the Eastern Stars, the Women's Catholic Auxiliary group in Jasper, Eleanor Case Board in Edmonton, and the Jasper Healthcare Foundation. Once, twin girls organized their birthday party as a fundraiser for our cause. They asked that instead of presents, monetary gifts be given to support our miracle mission. You can imagine how much my heart expanded as a result of all these gifts.

Despite the picture painted by the media, there are many incredible, generous people alive today.

How to execute the best Fun(d)raiser for you

1. Make a list of what you like to do. Are you a person who likes to entertain, be outside, work with a group, work by yourself, do you mind getting your hands dirty? Be honest. The more things you can come up with the better.
2. What are some of your natural talents? Are you a good speaker? A good organizer? Good with technology? Are you handy? Can you paint? The idea here is that you are going to make the money you need easily.
3. What does your network like to do? Do you socialize with golfers? Bike racers? Performers? Painters? Do your friends have a thing for cars? Hunting? Hockey? Knitting? You can build a fun(d)raiser around anything. All you need is …
4. Creativity!!! Be as flexible and creative as you can. Whatever ideas you can imagine, try them! Even if it's something that has never been done before,

"the Power of the Universe will come to your assistance if your heart and mind are in Unity."[5]

5. Involve people who can help you. The more people you can engage in your 'Miracle in Motion' the better for you. Please know that the people you attract will feel involved in something wonderful and that will give them something their heart wants. You know this, when we can be of service it feels good. You can give people that experience.

6. Give yourself enough time to organize your event.

7. Have fun!!! I cannot stress this enough... *only* do things that will make you smile, laugh, feel like you are having a little holiday from your life. Every month for two years, I ran an Improv night for the local youth. I would laugh so hard at each of these events it was like a dose of happiness that would keep me going for the next month. We made money, and I got a boost.

A Course in Miracles says, "To give, is to receive." For me, everyone who contributed to our cause became, and still are, part of the Miracle in Motion team. To me, every donation counted, whether it was small or large. I felt the energy around our project grow. Suddenly we weren't alone anymore. We truly were part of a community. And community, as far as I'm concerned, ROCKS!!!

A "lit" community is a healthy community. A healthy community creates miracles. A community formed on miracles heals our Earth. See how these kids activate love? Oh, they are sneaky little creatures, but smart as heck!!!

Awe * tis * (th)em

---

[5] White Buffalo Calf Woman

Chapter 8—Trust Yourself

Perhaps I should have started with this chapter, but somehow I don't think I would have gotten your attention. "Trust yourself," you say? "How do I do that?" Through experience. Through listening (or not) to that part of yourself that does truly know what is best to do. With countless decisions to make, you will probably find that sometimes you listen to yourself and at other times, not. If you pay attention, you will notice when you listened and it paid off in your favour, and when you didn't and you paid. Sometimes in a big way. Trust me; I have encountered both scenarios.

Extreme Sports

Over the course of our program, I taught Julianne to downhill ski, ride a two-wheeler bicycle and I enrolled her in horseback riding. Some people thought I was crazy. "What if she hits a tree?" they would say. Or, worse yet, "What if she breaks her neck, arm, leg?" It was a process. It took four years to teach Julianne to downhill ski. When we first started, we would sometimes last on the baby hill for ten minutes. She would throw her hands up in the sky and scream "I'm done." We packed up our stuff and left the hill.

As she moved through the stages I wrote about in Chapter Three, my approach changed because she was at a point in her development where I could ask for more. "We are going to do three runs today" I would say. By this point, we were riding the chair lift up Marmot Basin in our beautiful Jasper Mountain home. Often Jewels would try to get out of the third run and head towards the chalet. I would stay firm on completing the three runs because that was the expectation laid out at the beginning of the day. My experience with this approach with people with autism has been very successful. It gives them a beginning and an end. This concept was thoroughly outlined to us by our Superhero, Jonathan Alderson. Remember, though, timing is everything.

Today, Jewels is completely in control and loves to ski. Next year she will start up with the Special Olympics downhill program in Calgary. I get offers to work in ski schools all the time. How did I do it? Patience and trust. Plus, I watched all the other ski instructors and used their teaching methods. I even learned how to ski backwards!

Julianne riding a two-wheeler was a trip I will always remember. I would get so frustrated with her because she would pedal a few times and then throw her bike down. I practiced the art of patience and breathing like I had never known.

Every angry thought and word that came up in my brain, I passively listened to and viewed as if I was observing someone else. When the storm in my mind would stop, my consciousness would be drawn to something beautiful—a flower, a mountain, or a deer in the distance. I would look at Julianne as if nothing had happened and would say, "Okay let's ride again."

This "ride and stop" behaviour occurred for one week. It took everything I had to keep going. Each "stop" was the same for me: I was allowing myself to "see" the dark parts within me. Once they were seen and heard, they vanished. I wasn't stuffing them back down into my subconscious mind anymore. I wanted them freed. So long as they were not hurting anyone, all was well.

Being an observer of my shadow was very healing. One day Jewels jumped on her two-wheeler and rode. Rode like the wind. Another way for her to feel free. And after all that "release", there was more light in Mom.

Horseback riding was equally satisfying for Jules. We were blessed to have a therapeutic riding program in Jasper for many years. Helen Van Tongeren was our archangel here. At first, Julianne was tentative and anxious around the horses. Under the careful eye of Helen, Julianne grew to love riding. I remember one specific day she was lying in her bed, and she put her hands behind her head and very contentedly said, "I love riding." Julianne Shea was in love.

As she zips down the ski hill, hands outstretched, I often hear her proclaim her love of skiing to the passing trees. Love running through my child's body is a good thing. The feelings of self-confidence she has from accomplishing these sports also feeds her soul. On our last ski trip this year, at Norquay in Banff, Alberta, she turned to me on the chairlift and said, "you know I'm a really good skier."

" I know," I said. Four years of work was well worth it!!!

TRUST

 In the deepest part of my guts, I knew she could do these things. I JUST KNEW.

Tools from the Toolbox

Just after returning from three months in Mexico with Julianne, I was invited to join a group of people who were presenting at the Autism ONE conference in Chicago. Needless to say, my financial situation wasn't abundant then. However, I experienced that familiar feeling that I should attend. The voice was clear: "GO!" Jenny

McCarthy was presenting at the conference, and I wanted to give her a DVD copy of the musical I had co-written, celebrating our children with autism.

My son offered to take care of Julianne and drive her back to Jasper while my caregivers there confirmed they would assist her while I was away. So, full steam ahead. I arrived at Edmonton airport at 6am to find that there was one remaining ticket to Chicago on the flight that would be leaving shortly. It was $1,200 for a return flight. I had to sit down. $1,200 for me at this time was an enormous amount of money. I had just taken three months off to work with Julianne in Mexico. I was expecting the price to be much less.

My gut was telling me to go, but the angst inside was telling me "NO". I decided to use a technique I learned from Edward de Bono that made my decision 100% clear. I returned to the counter, purchased my ticket and boarded the plane. Of course, I made it through the next couple of months financially. Some miracles occurred, and I mean this sincerely. When we believe in miracles, they can and will occur. The biggest miracle that came out of this experience was to always trust myself. I learned I can and always will be able to make money. Money is in constant flow. As long as I am willing to do something, give something, money will come. My belief is "I always have enough" and by some strange coincidence, I always do. Sometimes "enough" is exactly down to the last penny but it is there, nonetheless.

The exercise that got me on the plane is a simple one that Edward de Bono shares in his book *The Six Thinking Hats*. Often, when faced with a seemingly difficult situation, we square off the positive points against the negative ones as in a chess game. As we have all experienced, this doesn't always simplify our decision-making process. He suggests that you add a third category to your process. The title of this column will read " What will be interesting if I do or don't do X?" It is in this category that we often uncover where our fears exist. It is then up to you to decide whether you want to override your fear(s) or not. In my case, I choose to conquer them, and I am so grateful that I did.

Trust

People with autism are supposed to love routine. For the most part they do but, for whatever reason, my Julianne loves to travel. I have learned this over the course of time. Mention the words trip, travel or airplane to her and her beautiful face lights up like a pumpkin on Halloween. First, I took her on small trips and one-week holidays, and every time without fail she learned some new skill along the way. I remember her drawing her first letter "c" in San Diego airport at 4am.

In the Dominican Republic, because of her experience with therapeutic riding which I mentioned earlier, she rode her own horse on a trail ride we all went on. At an evening beach party, she stood up under her own volition and sang Ottawa's "Hands Up (Give Me Your Heart)" song, with the other kids. She won at bingo and easily walked up on stage to accept her prize.

A little baffling, but real.

All well and good. One week out of her routine—no big deal. Deciding to take Jewels to Europe for five weeks, however, required a significant amount of trust. There are so many wonder-filled stories I would love to share from this and the following year's five-week trip. I could probably write a whole book series called "Where In The World Is Julianne Now?" Julianne, my friend Helen, and I, cherish the memories of these journeys as if they were gold itself.

Again, many people questioned my mental health regarding these choices. What I will say here and now, though, is that the Earth undoubtedly experienced large influxes of love as three little tourists drove six thousand kilometers through France, Italy, Switzerland, Greece and Germany. Julianne was so much fun! Every town we visited treated us like royalty. We had people escorting us to places (this was in the days before affordable GPS). "Follow us," they'd say. "We will take you there." At the statue of David in Florence, we were waved in as if they were expecting us, allowing us to bypass the two-hour line-up. Even Helen asked us, "Who are you guys?" People in a French Restaurant offered Julianne the food they had ordered; just handed her the plate saying, "Welcome to Chartres, France." It was unbelievable!

I could entertain you with story after story. All in all, I encourage you to listen to your voice, gut, feelings, and knowing, as by doing so it will bring great bliss to your life, and you are entitled to that. In *A Course in Miracles*, it explains, "I am entitled to miracles."

You so surely are.

We were on our way back from our first trip. Just as the plane was about to land in Edmonton, Julianne bent forward from her seat. I followed her actions whilst hoping she wasn't going to throw up, and she leaned into me and almost in a whisper said, "Thank you." Her words permeated my soul. I knew exactly what she was saying. *Thank you Mom, for allowing me this joyous experience and thank you for trusting me.* Such sincerity. I cried.

Consequences of Not Listening

I wish I could say that all our trips created such love and harmony. I can't. One, in particular, turned into a most challenging time for both Julianne and me. To be completely honest, it was probably the scariest time of my life.

This story evolves around pharmaceutical drugs, and me as Momma Bear, not listening. The experience led us down a rabbit hole so deep, I was afraid I might hurt my child. After all we had gone through, this was not the way our story was going to end. This much I promised myself.

It all began on our second trip to Europe. We started to notice some erratic behaviour on Julianne's part. Although she still enjoyed all the cathedrals and art galleries, restaurants seemed to cause her stress. I coped with this behaviour by picnicking with her as much as possible, which helped. Something was different though, but I couldn't quite put my finger on it.

When we returned home, we moved into our new apartment. At school, Julianne had a new aid.

Her behaviour worsened and for the first time, I sought help from the medical community. Julianne was prescribed Ativan, and she got worse. The dosage was increased and she got even worse. An antidepressant was added and, she got worse still. We switched out the antidepressant for an antipsychotic. Worse. We threw in sleeping pills—Valium—and SHE STILL GOT WORSE!

Julianne had transformed into an Avatar-type being with the strength of ten men and the speed of an antelope. She did not sleep. She was irritable. She was frustrated. In a nutshell, she was EXHAUSTING.

I didn't sleep for three weeks. She didn't sleep for three weeks. It was a nightmare. Even though I used every tool I had to keep myself balanced, I wasn't doing very well. Many people in my community came up to me, and said, "This is too much for you... too much." I resorted to locking myself in my bathroom at night just to get some distance from her. Upon hearing this, my good friend Jacinta Broemeling, who is also a nurse; said: "Grace, this is not healthy."

One night, I had a momentary vision of me putting my hands around her neck and for two minutes suffocating her, and I burst into tears. "Oh my God", I realized. "I am a threat to my daughter." I wept, copious tears streaming down my face. I couldn't believe this was happening to us.

Enough feeling sorry for myself, I thought. Even though I knew I might lose guardianship over Julianne, I knew that my nervous system had been stressed to such a point that I had to make a change in our living arrangements. I had to have distance between us or something terrible could occur.

I knew that, with my last bit of strength, I had to make her safe. It was my duty. And so, at 4am on November 16th, I packed two suitcases. One for her, one for me.

The Universe had other plans, however. On the very day that I decided to arrange for the distance between us, packed our suitcases and was determined to drive to a major center, there was an enormous snow storm. All roads leading out of town were closed.

Now, what? We had been to the hospital many times over the past few weeks, so I decided to call 911 because that's what I knew to do. They instructed me to go to the hospital. Julianne was escorted in and admitted. A specialist in Edmonton was contacted, and the doctor on call was told to pull her off all the medications she was currently on and sedate her.

It was a very challenging time.

Julianne was like a wild animal. I still have video footage of her on the ground. The doctors tried numerous sedations and finally one "that would put a horse down for three days" was administered to her. Twenty-four hours later she woke up and walked the halls of the hospital. We were all scared. What would happen next? Everyone who knew her came and walked with her. Our excellent local massage therapist took on the midnight to 4am shift. Our local chiropractor, Dr. Peter, spent the wee hours of the morning from 4am to 8am beside her in the hospital. My Family of Light, that I spoke of earlier, boarded buses in Prince George. They drove up from Edmonton. The troops came.

Our local Community Outreach Services group assisted me and called our social worker.

"Why didn't you call me?" she asked.

It honestly had not crossed my mine. And so I realized that when a person is so maxed out, their nervous system so stretched, they lose cognitive skills. I now understand how people hurt their children. I came too close for comfort. I have no judgment on these "crimes" any longer.

Over the next few days, I spoke with an excellent psychiatrist from the Ponoka mental health center. She apologized for what we had to go through. She assured me Julianne would recalibrate, but it would take time, and the detox process would be ugly. She drew a picture of what I could expect and she was correct. It was a very disturbing four months, watching my daughter revert to behaviours she exhibited at seven years old.

All the work we had done over the years was nowhere to be seen. Gone. Vanished. Vamoose.

I had to dig deep to trust that somewhere in her she would still have all her skills, tucked away and protected. In time, I chose to believe she would regain them all. I am happy to announce that she did. But it took time. This was a huge learning for me. I have asked myself in hindsight, *What was I thinking?* Why did I so blindly trust in a system without checking their recommendations? After all, I could have. I had tools in my toolbox to do that, but I didn't. I totally gave over my power. Why?

According to a teacher of mine named Tom Kenyon, we had entered into a Chaotic planetary node at the time all this was happening to us. Well, I can certainly attest to that. Chaos ruled supreme. In the end, I have forgiven myself for the error I made in not checking in with my tools. Sometimes we make mistakes; sometimes we make big, big mistakes and with forgiveness, we move forward. I think of the Mary Poppins song—"a spoon full of sugar helps the medicine go down."

Picking Up The Pieces

Today, just over two years after this incident, all is well.

Julianne now lives with her Dad and is very happy. She loves her Papa very much, and it's good for them to spend time together. We see each other monthly, and she now has a cell phone so we can text anytime we choose. Or Skype.

So that's how it works my friends. What I have learned over the course of twenty years is that when I do listen to my internal *knowing*, I most often experience *joy*. When I don't, I don't. To this day, sometimes my logical mind will kick in and try and coerce me into not listening to my *knowingness*. Because of experience, I thank it for its opinion and choose instead to listen to the knowingness. But like all of us, I am still learning. Sometimes, I still mess up. And that's OK too, because we are all learning. Every one of us. One big soup of humanity is learning.

As I mentioned earlier in this book, I had an experience of automatic writing when I was seventeen years old, when I was cautioned to "Pick your tools wisely, and you will survive." All I would add to this sentiment is "… and thrive."

Trusting yourself is a wise tool. Use it.

Afterword

Thank you for reading this book. It is my hope that the words on these pages have inspired you, helped you, comforted you and perhaps even challenged you. I want you to know you are not alone. There are many of us veterans now who are here to help you. Please trust yourself enough to reach out to us if you need help.

We have been in your shoes, walked your same path. We have cried and screamed, raged and begged. We have wished this was not our life. We actually understand this journey. As I can only speak for myself, I have found peace. I have felt the *AWE* in autism. I am profoundly grateful (as difficult as it was) for the journey I had with my Jewel. I cannot think of anything that would have changed me so dramatically in twenty years.

On the www.childrenofautumn.com website, you can visit our current offerings, as well as our blog titled Where in the World is Julianne now?

At http://childrenofautumn.com/book-resources/ you will find an introduction to the *Children of Autumn* musical. Should you, or anyone you know, wish to produce it in your hometown, please contact us..

It has been my honour to spend this time with you. I pray for many miracles for you and your family. I encourage you to have faith that every experience is there to help you grow your own light. Accept the lesson that when things don't go your way, something more important to the growth of your soul is in the works. Remember: when you stay connected to your spiritual core, the best and most advantageous path unfolds. Keep your eyes focused on that which you are becoming. A beacon, an inspiration, a love beam.

0 1341 1660530 1

CPSIA information can be obtained
at www.ICGtesting.com
Printed in the USA
FFOW04n1506210617
36997FF

9 781535 281904